AT THE END OF THE ROAD

One man's journey from chaos to clarity

Tim White

WITH KIMBERLY M. SMITH

Tim White Ministries

© 2012 by Timothy H. White
ISBN 978-0-9859177-0-8
LCCN 2012917630

When at the end of the road, we find that we can no longer function as a human being, either with or without drugs, we all face the same dilemma. What is there left to do? There seems to be this alternative: either go on as best we can to the bitter ends—jails, institutions, or death—or find a new way to live. In years gone by, very few addicts ever had this last choice. Those who are addicted today are more fortunate. For the first time in man's entire history, a simple way has been proving itself in the lives of many addicts. It is available to us all. This is a simple, spiritual—not religious—program, known as Narcotics Anonymous.

From the White Booklet,
Narcotics Anonymous

CONTENTS

Authors' Notes

AUTHOR'S NOTE

This is a work of nonfiction. While memory is a tricky thing, all events, experiences, actions, and their consequences have been faithfully retold herein as I have remembered them. Care has been taken to change the names and identifying characteristics of certain individuals.

Conversations presented in dialogue form have been recreated from my best recollection and are not intended as a word-for-word account of what was said but, rather, to communicate the general spirit of the conversation.

This work represents my personal truth and my struggle from a confused child to a man in recovery, a man experiencing clarity for the first time in his life. My hope is that my story may start others who are struggling in confusion and anger, locked in the stronghold of addiction, down the path of clarity and recovery. If my life is a testament to anything, it is that it is never too late.

COAUTHOR'S NOTE

From time to time, we are presented opportunities to make a difference—those occasions when the stars align, the Spirit of the Universe, which many of us choose to call God, and life circumstances come together to bless us with a chance to do good and powerful work. Such a moment came for me when I received an e-mail in late August of 2011 from Tim White's brother Billy Boston. I will be eternally grateful to Billy for reaching out to me. The opportunity to help Tim share his story with the world has touched me in ways deeply personal and immensely enriching.

On December 22, 2002, my mother entered the home of my eldest brother, Curtis Wilson Smith, to find him deceased, surrounded by numerous consumed bottles of alcohol and a pill bottle of prescription drugs. He was forty-seven. An intense intellectual, creative writer and musician, and lover of animals, art, and nature, Curtis was loved and admired by many friends and our family. He was also, from an early age, an alcoholic and a troubled, complex man.

I lay this all on the line to make known to the readers of this memoir that addiction affects the lives of many—as it has my life and the lives of my family and friends—and that it is a powerful and cunning disease.

Tim's story is, in many ways, my brother's story. It is the story of the addict, in whatever forms his or her addiction rears its ugly head. In a broader sense, it is the story of all our loved ones who find themselves lost in their addictions. Gratefully, it is also a story of hope, recovery, healing, and love. It is a story of faith and forward motion.

I thank Tim White and his family for allowing me the true privilege to do this work. I have taken great care to remain faithful to Tim's voice and the account of his journey. Through this process, I've come to find the courage to face my own addiction with an eating disorder and to begin the work of recovery. Even before its publication, Tim's story has touched lives and brought about positive results. May it continue to do so.

INTRODUCTION

Living in the Madness: Jacksonville, 1968

A FAMILIAR PANIC GRABBED HOLD OF ME. Even at six years old, I knew from his first beer that night what madness was to come. What had been the cause this time? The initiating incident, the erupting spark? Now, I couldn't say. I don't know if I even knew then. To be honest, it could have been anything. Like Daddy's drinking and drugging, the madness was just there. Like everyday life, like a chronic sickness, like the air.

Even when things seemed calm, the madness was there. Always.

Daddy turned on a dime, a dime as thin as the ones I'd bummed from the men in the bar next to Grandma's house. Not this house, the one I was in now at six years old, in a rough section of Jacksonville, Florida, referred to by the locals as Sin City. But the last house, downtown, off 8th Street, next to the bar where young and old men alike drank and tossed me dimes when Daddy took me in to visit his friend, the owner and bartender. Sometimes the men fought each other outside, along the brick wall that faced the house. I watched entertained by their drunken swings and punches, their occasional missed contacts that caused them to stumble or fall on the hard ground.

Those men's drunken antics could be funny, but nothing was entertaining about the madness or about Daddy that night as I tried to stay small, quiet, and out of his way, panicked about what might come next. Fear swelled in me as their shouts grew louder. Grandma, her friend Lester Case, who lived with us most of the time, Uncle David, and Daddy—the whole lot of them—threw words and insults at one another like daggers, meant to strike deep.

I tried to stay away from them, but they moved around the house, following one another, continuing the chaos. Even covering my ears was no escape from the shouts and confusion.

Daddy was a mean drunk. Though I can't remember exactly what he said that night, it seemed to me that he was meaner than usual—vicious and spiteful in his attacks. Unable to escape the madness inside the house, I bolted for the back door.

My mother, who lived with my four older half brothers on the other side of town, had taught me the thing to do when you needed help was get on your knees and ask God for it. Dressed in only my underwear, I ran for the back door, swinging it open with all the strength in my young body.

I dashed down the back steps. The damp grass felt cool under my bare feet. Halfway to the back fence, next to the home-rigged cement block swimming pool, I fell to my knees and turned my face to the night sky. All I could think was that I needed to pray. God would help me. I don't remember if I had full confidence in his help at that particular moment, but, for my part, I was going to do my best to ask in the most proper way my young brain could figure: on my knees and with an earnestness right up there with the preachers and the nicest of my Sunday school teachers.

Stars twinkled like tiny fires in the clear night sky. A warm breeze blew across my face. I clutched my hands in prayer as I'd been taught, face to the starlit sky. Surely God would hear me, hear the sincerity in my voice, the need.

"Dear God, help me!" I shouted into the night.

Tears ran down my face. I didn't wipe them away. It was okay if tears wet my whole face and my nose ran, if only God helped end the madness.

"Lord Jesus," I cried out, "please stop them. Please make it quit."

I don't remember how long I stayed in my grandmother's backyard, on my knees and dressed in only my underwear, or how long I prayed that night for God to strip away the madness and settle the constant storm that was my life. At some point, I must have gotten up, gone back inside the house, and put myself to bed, but I've no memory of it.

I remember being afraid, the confusion and yelling and craziness of it all. I remember turning my face up to the sky, melting in tears, pleading for God to intervene and make things good. I remember my six-year-old small voice, straining to make it sound big so God would hear and answer my prayers, calling out to heaven, "Please, Lord Jesus, save me! This ain't right!"

Even as a young boy I knew, *this ain't right*. Nothing in my life at that point—or for the next twenty-six years—would feel right. I was living in the madness, and a life of calm and clarity was decades away.

But, it would come.

At thirty-one, the confusion of my life would fall away. The questions that plagued me to that point would be answered: What's happening to me? Where do I fit in? Why am I here? I would no longer be that scared little boy in Grandma's backyard, but a man who had found his way, led by a higher power to the road of recovery.

This account represents my struggle with the early trauma of a life lived in chaos and confusion, my resulting resentment and anger, my battles with drugs, alcohol, and the law, and the clarity I found in recovery. I approach this retelling of events not as one who was so strong and special he could overcome such daunting obstacles, but as one so weakened and humbled by the pain and suffering I both felt and imposed on others that I had nowhere else to turn but to God and the sanity found in treatment and recovery.

My message is a simple but powerful one, offered without ego, pride, or self-importance, for anyone living in the madness or who loves someone seemingly lost to it: *It's never too late.*

No matter the road on which we find ourselves or how far we stray from any clear direction, it's never too late to turn things around. At the end of the road is a new path forward—if only we open ourselves to it. The way forward—to a new road and a new beginning—is simple: *one step at a time.*

Adversity is the diamond
dust Heaven polishes its jewels with.
THOMAS CARLYLE

CHAPTER 1

February 1993: Part 1

THE SOUND OF THE STEEL DOORS, ROLLING METAL on metal, rang in my ears as I lined up with the other inmates incarcerated in the Duval County Jail. Here I was again, locked up, this time for violation of probation in connection with petty theft charges I'd racked up in the throes of another drug and alcohol relapse. At thirty-one years old, I'd been locked up in jail or prison, driven into detox and addiction treatment, or lost on the streets for most of my adult life.

What made this time different, at least this time behind bars, was that I'd turned myself in. Three weeks of waiting and I was standing in line to be escorted to the courthouse holding cell where I'd face Judge Walker and learn my sentence. I was tired and sick and, more than anything, ready to be done with it.

The sentence I'd get from Judge Walker, if anything above and beyond time served, would be light, a cake walk. I'd been before Walker numerous times for various offenses. Inmates called her "Walking Walker." She was known to be lenient and had always treated me kindly. A slight, older woman with thick black eyeglasses, she reminded me of someone's granny. She might scold, but she wasn't going to throw the book at you. She was no hard ass, like some other judges I'd known or heard of. After all, I'd given myself up, I figured.

In some bout of morality, I'd scraped together the last bits of human decency left in me and turned myself in so that my mother would not lose her travel trailer to the bail bondsman. I'd done so much already, wrecked every relationship I had and put everyone I cared about, and a bunch I didn't, through living hell. Now, I was turning myself in, doing the right thing. Surely, Judge Walker would take that into account.

I sat in the holding cell waiting for the bailiff to call the court to order. From previous trips before judges, I knew my public defender, who I hadn't even met as of yet, and the district attorney's lawyer would plead out my case. It wasn't like I was claiming innocence. I was guilty, though guilt wasn't an emotion I felt a lot of back then, at least by this time. Mostly, I was numb. Detached. Worn out. All the years of fighting to dodge my dad's anger, suppress my pain with alcohol and drugs, and manipulate situations to get my needs met had left me empty. No public defender or DA or county judge could do more harm to me than I'd done to myself.

Court in session, I waited. I'd be fine, I told myself. Judge Walker would go easy on me. As I waited to hear my name called, though, an uneasy feeling stirred in the pit of my stomach. The longer it took to hear my name, the more my nerves unraveled.

My heart skipped a beat when the deep voice of the bailiff called out, "Timothy Houston White."

Guards entered the holding cell and walked me out to stand before "Walking Walker."

Instantly, I sensed something was wrong.

Judge Walker leaned forward in her seat as I entered the courtroom. When I made eye contact with her, the muscles in her thin face tensed and her eyes narrowed. Her expression told me she was upset. By the way she glared at me, I knew her mood had much to do with me. My hands began to sweat. A panic rose from my gut. This wasn't good.

I looked over at my court-appointed attorney. A young guy, he seemed green and inexperienced. The bad feeling in my gut growing, I walked forward and stood next to him at the defense table. Leaning toward me, he whispered, "Nine months."

Nine months? What had happened to Walking Walker? What was this judge thinking? I'd turned myself in, for Christ's sake. Didn't that count for something?

The panic spread through my body. Standing at the defendant's table next to my wimp of a public defender, I was a child all over again, searching my mind for a way to skirt out of harm's way, to find an escape. Nine months? I couldn't do nine more months locked up. I could use a short rest from the drinking and drugging, some time to let things settle down, get people back on my side maybe, but *nine months*? What the hell were these fools thinking?

"Let me talk to the judge," I whispered back to my attorney.

"She's decided," he said matter-of-factly. "She doesn't want to hear from you."

I leaned against the wood table. "I want to talk to the judge, to address the court," I said, louder this time.

Ignoring my attorney's protests, I turned to Judge Walker. "Your Honor, may I please address the court?"

I'd no idea what I planned to say. All I knew was that I had that one moment to sway the judge and change this outcome. I had to do something, pull some rabbit out of a hat.

Judge Walker squinted harder. Her stare felt like a laser slicing my insides, but it didn't silence me or keep me from doing what had to be done.

"Your Honor," I continued, "if you'll let me address the court—"

Judge Walker's expression turned to anger as she cut me short, "No, Mr. White, you may not. You have been nothing but a pain in my side for years."

Her words floored me. This judge had always been kind to me, had seemed to understand my circumstances. Where was this coming from? Briefly, I wondered if I'd used up even the good graces of kindly Judge Walker, as I'd used up the graces and patience of everyone else in my life. Then, the moment passed. I couldn't consider that now. I dug in even firmer.

"But, Your Honor," I cried out, "I'm sick. I'm an alcoholic and drug addict. I need help, Your Honor."

I have no idea where the words came from. Perhaps from a place that exists deep within all scared and confused creatures, a place where survival mode kicks in. Or maybe I'd grown into such a supreme con artist that I was capable of concocting wild but believable stories at the drop of a hat.

15

In either case, what poured out from me was pure genius, so real seeming that it wasn't long at all, minutes maybe, before I began believing my own sad story. Of course, it was all a lie.

I threw my hands in the air and leaned over the defense table. "Your Honor, I've been accepted into inpatient treatment at Gateway Community Services. If only you'll agree." I pretended to look around the room, as if searching for someone from the treatment center. "There was supposed to be someone from the Substance Abuse Program Office here."

I knew all the right things to say, all the correct lingo and department names. Why wouldn't I? I'd been an alcoholic and crack addict for years, in and out of rehab. There wasn't a program or related government office in town that I didn't have some working knowledge of. I didn't know if my scam would work on the court, but at least I was fairly sure I could make it sound good.

My public defender looked at me as if I'd gone slap crazy. The attorney from the DA's office whispered to his assistant, and members of the courtroom audience joined me in scanning the room for the missing Substance Abuse Program representative.

I had them hooked.

Even though I'd worked myself into a severe panic by playing the part I'd fabricated, I did my best to engage the judge in eye contact. She was my ticket out of this mess. She still seemed upset with me, as I gave her the best "poor me" look I could muster.

Locked in our own private struggle, the judge and I stared at one another. After a long minute of silence, her face slackened and her shoulders relaxed. I held my breath and waited for what would come next.

Judge Walker shifted in her chair and said, "Well, why aren't they here?"

"I don't know, Your Honor," I pleaded, wringing my hands. I could tell I was gaining ground with her, but I didn't want to overdo it, so I tempered my actions and waited for her reply. Beside me, I heard my attorney take a deep breath and sigh. Obviously, he hadn't counted on such theatrics, but he must have known there was no way of stopping things now. The public defender could sigh all he wanted; I kept my eyes on the judge.

Judge Walker hesitated, then said, "Take him back to the holding cell. I want somebody from Substance Abuse brought in here now."

Score. Mark up one for my side.

Somehow, I'd been able to talk my way, once again, out of a sticky situation.

But, my sense of accomplishment would be short-lived. While the guards took me back to the holding cell, an unavoidable realization washed over me: my story was pure crap, and it was only a matter of time before the judge would find out the truth. No one was coming from Substance Abuse to help me. No one gave a darn if I did nine months in jail, or returned to prison, or overdosed on the streets of Jacksonville, Florida.

By the time I made it to the cell, I'd plunged back into the blackness that had become my life. The judge would find out I'd made the whole thing up, and then what would she do? I'd only made matters worse, spinning a web of lies I couldn't step out of now. I paced the holding cell and wracked my brain for a way out of the mess I'd created.

It wasn't long before the bailiff called my name for a second time that day.

Walking into the courtroom, my attention focused immediately on a large, middle-aged lady sitting at the DA's table. I didn't remember her from earlier. As I made my way up the aisle, the woman shuffled a stack of folders. I shifted position so I'd be close to her as we got to the front of the courtroom. I figured she was hunting a folder with my name on it. Of course, I knew there wasn't one, but something inside me hoped, maybe half expected, a folder labeled *Timothy H. White* might appear out of nowhere, as if by magic.

Once facing Judge Walker, I looked over at the DA's table and asked, "Where's my folder?" Before the lady could answer, I turned my attention to the judge and, with my best expression of confusion and anguish, said, "I don't know what's happening, Your Honor."

I could hear the lady still looking through her files, the thick manila folders sliding one across the other. My mind flashed on the rolling steel jail doors. I was seconds away from the judge's sentence. I could feel it. Judge Walker's eyes were on me as I fixed on her, my whole being pleading for mercy, hoping against hope that I'd slide out of my current predicament.

Judge Walker looked down on me from her seat on the raised platform. A soft sigh escaped her lips as she removed her glasses from her face and laid them on her bench. "Mr. White, I'm sentencing you to ninety days in

Gateway inpatient treatment to begin immediately."

I was stunned.

"Thank you, Your Honor," I said, trying to gain my composure.

On the way back to jail, where I'd await transport to treatment, I tried figuring out how I'd managed to pull off such a tremendous con. This would be my third stint in Gateway Community Services and rehab. By now, I was practically a pro at treatment, knew just what to say and do to get through.

I'd fooled the court and would probably fool the rehab crowd, but there was no fooling myself. I was an alcoholic and addict and no amount of treatment was going to help me. I was a trapped rat—imprisoned in a maze with no way out, forever racing down one path, then another, destined, eventually, to accept its fate and give up.

I'd do a few months at Gateway and then be back on the streets, back to the addictions, back to my life of darkness and madness and misery. I was a hopeless case, beyond help. Too far down the road of ruin to be good for anything or anyone. Judge Walker had shown me a little mercy, but I knew I deserved none from myself.

A childhood filled with confusion and anger had taught me how to manipulate others—first out of self-protection, then out of self-centeredness and self-destruction. Now, I'd pulled off the ultimate manipulation, a major scam on the system, and talked my way out of a jail sentence and into drug and alcohol treatment.

Too bad it was too late.

And He took the children in His
arms, put His hands on them
and blessed them.

MARK 10:16

CHAPTER 2

Enter Timothy

WE'D ALL LIKE TO BELIEVE THE DAY WE ENTERED THE world trumpets sounded, announcements arrived, celebrations began. I think it's safe to say that we'd all love to know, to *really* know—to feel it deep down in our souls—that we came into this world wanted, anticipated, received with joy. I wish I could say that.

I suspect there was little fanfare February 3, 1962, for Yvonne Louise White and her newborn son. I don't know who was at the hospital to support my mother or greet me on my first day out. I know my father, Houston White, was in a German hospital trying to kick an addiction to heroin.

When I became an adult, my father would tell me of his joy in getting the phone call that his wife back in the States had given birth to his son, first and only—and on his own birthday no less. He was thirty-four, a Merchant Marine, away from home most of the time, and an alcoholic and drug addict. Maybe that's why he'd been in the hospital trying to kick the habit—because I was on the way. Maybe he'd imagined a stable life with my mom, me, and my four older half brothers. He didn't say it explicitly, which wasn't unusual in my family, as little was ever explained or discussed. I know whatever he tried at that German hospital didn't work, at least not for long. He was never successful in getting off drugs and alcohol and died an addict, hooked up to an oxygen tank, the result of years of cigarette smoking and abuse to his body.

All this isn't to say "poor pitiful me." Far from it. From an early age, I knew there were folks who loved me, especially my grandma, my father's mother, who spent the most time raising me. And every mistake I've made or harm I've caused, I own. I recognize the love I received. By no means was my life always bad. Yet, we are formed from the stuff of our early memories—there's no way around that fact—and shaking off a bad start can be harder for some than others. I suppose it took me a great deal longer than it should have, longer than most maybe, to move past it.

THE FIRST IMAGE I REMEMBER OF MY FATHER IS OF HIS exiting a yellow checker taxi, fresh home from sea. We lived in downtown Jacksonville, on 8th Street, in a two-story wood frame house Dad had rented for Grandma and me.

From the front window, I watched my father open the taxicab door, dressed in a sharp-looking suit, smiling from ear to ear. I scampered out the door and down the front porch steps in a flash. I remember how he scooped me up and held me in his arms. The feeling was amazing, and I loved him back then.

Daddy was like Superman to me. Though he wasn't tall, standing only five-eight, his broad shoulders and stocky build made for a formidable appearance. With his movie-star looks and deep, strong voice, he took over a room. Everyone seemed drawn to him. When he was in a good mood, I loved being near him. When he wasn't, I did everything to stay away.

With four boys already from two previous marriages, Mom had too much on her hands and too few resources. Of course, what I know of my mother's circumstances I've pieced together over the years, here and there, bit by bit. Things were never fully explained to me. My earliest memories are of living with my grandmother, Edith White.

Grandma White had two sons, David and Houston. My grandfather died before I was born, so I've no memory of him. From all accounts, they had a happy marriage, though my grandfather had done a ten-year stretch in prison for, what little was explained to me, something to do with taxes.

22

Dad's older brother always lived nearby but not with us. Sometimes Lester Case, Grandma's "friend," stayed with us. Mostly, it was Grandma and me.

Often, when we lived on 8th Street, she'd walk me to the movie theatre downtown, The Center, buy me a ticket, and sit me down in the theatre with explicit instructions not to leave. And, I wouldn't, no matter what. She'd leave to do her shopping—back when a person could do all her necessary shopping downtown—and I'd watch the movie, scared to get up, even to go to the bathroom, for fear she'd return and find me missing. Sometimes, I'd worry if she'd return. Of course, she'd always return, and we'd walk home together, me helping carry the bags.

Grandma never drove a car or held a paying job. Daddy gave her money to take care of me. From what I gather, he was her main source of financial support. Time would prove that it would become Dad's habit to pay people to raise me.

Life on 8th Street had some good times, but even those were short lived. Daddy would come home, mostly smiling and in a good mood, but his smile wouldn't last. It was never long before my Dad and Grandma would go at it. I've never seen two people, still to this day, who seemed to both love and hate one another as fiercely as those two. Invariably, something would be said by one or the other—to start the bickering. Soon, the argument would escalate into cursing and objects being broken or thrown across the room. Sometimes it would get so bad that Grandma would call the police or run from the house, most often leaving me there, scared and alone with him.

The next day, things would go back to as they had been before the big fight, and nothing would ever be said of the incident. There was never the classic "making up" between the two of them. I never heard him apologize or try to set things straight. No heartfelt confessions and promises to do better made at the kitchen table the next morning. Just silence—almost as if he'd no awareness of the trouble and harm he'd caused. As if he'd forgotten, which was something I—and I suppose Grandma—could never do.

That's how it would go with my father for as long as I can remember: coming home, starting good, yelling and cussing, fighting and then forgetting, then more fighting and more forgetting. Then he would leave.

I wasn't too old, four or five maybe, when I began to look forward to his being away, out to sea. Life got better then.

But, he would always come home.

THE HOUSE ON 8TH STREET WASN'T THE ONLY HOME I KNEW back then—though it was the place I felt most secure and safe, between my father's bouts of violence. Sometimes, usually for short periods, I'd stay with my mother and brothers. At that time, my mother lived near her parents in Arlington, a middle-class neighborhood southeast of the St. Johns River.

My mother's parents helped raise and support her four older sons— Pete, Terry, Billy, and Mark. The oldest two, Pete and Terry, lived most often with Grandma and Granddaddy Taylor. Billy and Mark would live with my mother—wherever home for them was at the time—and I would live with Grandma White.

As I got older, I'd spend longer stretches living with my mother, or other folks my father paid to keep me, but those times would never prove to work out well. In the end, I'd always go back to Grandma's.

The biggest problem living with my mother was in my overwhelming feeling of being a boy out of place. Grandma White felt more like my mother than my own biological mother did. Not that my mother didn't try in her own way. Even with her parents' help, raising four boys— *five* when I was around—was no easy task. Someone always needed something, was into something. Even as a little boy, I could see how hard things were on my mother, how stressed—almost fragile—she seemed.

She'd been only twenty-five when she gave birth to me, a slender, part-Cherokee woman with glossy black hair, golden-brown eyes, and no luck in the men she'd chosen to marry. I tried not to need anything, not get in the way. I'd play with the boys outside when they wanted me to, but I never made a fuss to be cared for or have attention paid to me and learned quick from my father how to be polite and say "Yes, ma'am" and "No, sir."

What I loved about being with Mom was attending church. Church was always a fun time. The folks in church were nice and the music joyful. When I was lucky enough to be with Mom on a Sunday, we'd load up in Mom's car for Sunday school and services at Trinity Baptist Church. Sundays with Mom and my brothers made me feel more connected, to them and to the kind church folks. I wanted to be a part of what they offered.

I remember asking the preacher to *babatize me*—mispronouncing the word and making the grownups laugh.

One Sunday the preacher looked down at me, smiled, and said, "Didn't I baptize you last week?"

As far as I was concerned, dunking me underwater was a mess of fun, and afterwards the women hugged you and the men patted you on the back. I must have asked that preacher to *babatize me* a half-dozen times.

CHURCH WASN'T THE ONLY PLACE I LIKED BEING BACK then. I also had a fondness for the bar next to the house on 8th Street.

The bar was a dive, a typical "bucket of blood" sort of place. I liked the noise of the men talking over their drinks, swapping stories, laughing. Even when they looked out of sorts or wobbled when they stood to hit the can and unload, they seemed to be having fun. I found myself wanting to join in or, at the least, to grab their attention for a few fleeting seconds.

Dad would take me into the bar with him when he'd visit the owner. Being gone a lot, Dad didn't know all the men who hung out at the bar, but he seemed at ease there, maybe even more so than at home next door with me and Grandma. He was in a good mood when we were in the bar.

When I think back on it, I never should have been allowed there. Dad's friend was the owner and ran the place, pouring big mugs of beer from the tap for Dad and the other men, but who in their right mind drags their little kid into a bar, especially a cut-throat dive like that one? Now I know his addiction caused such lax judgment. I'd be guilty of poor judgment and insane thinking myself down the road. Today, I try not to dwell on such matters. Besides, I can imagine I might have begged to go with him a time or two.

The first money I ever bummed was in that bar. I don't recall how it started. I suppose a man, feeling fine off a few drinks, tossed me a dime or quarter and told me to enjoy myself. All I know is that I caught on quickly that folks would give you money if you asked the right way—and more money if you made them laugh or crack a smile. So, I'd pander to the drunks, telling jokes or smiling as I walked by. After a number of times in the bar and enough success in collecting change, I got comfortable enough to go right up and ask for any loose coins they could spare.

Dad never stopped me from bumming change, and I made it a point to make it easy on him to stay in the bar as long as he wanted. I don't remember how I spent the money or if I saved it up for a big present or treats from the grocery store, but I remember clearly how good it felt to get it. I'd make the men laugh, and they'd reach into their pockets or pluck a few coins from the table or bar top. I'd flash them a crooked smile and swiftly stash the coins in my pants pocket, thinking I'd gotten away with something fantastic.

Of course, my bumming money didn't end there at the bar at five years old. I'd go on to be an excellent beggar and scammer and, eventually, a plain ole thief. But it was early on, in those days at the 8th Street bar, that I learned the lucrative trade of fishing coins from pockets. Take and take and take: it was an impulse I'd grow all too familiar with—that and the impulse to place myself in surroundings teeming with drugs and alcohol.

I KNEW SOMETHING WAS TERRIBLY WRONG THE MOMENT I walked into the living room. Daddy lay slumped in the recliner, eyes rolled back in his head, tongue protruding in a way that seemed unnatural, frightening. His body shook, convulsing in spasms. Something straight out of a horror movie. I called for Grandma to hurry quick; something was wrong with Daddy.

"Ain't nothing wrong with your Daddy," Grandma said, "except he's on the dope."

Wide-eyed, I watched Daddy shake, a glob of saliva forming at the edge of his mouth. After a minute, he seemed to calm down, though he didn't come to but shifted his head away from me.

It was the first time I heard the word *dope*. It would be a few hundred more times I'd hear Grandma White call my father a "dope fiend," said matter-of-factly, as if were just the nature of things.

Grandma tried coaxing me out of the room. "He'll be all right. He'll sleep it off. Come in the kitchen and help me get supper ready."

I was glad he wasn't dying but shocked that we weren't calling the ambulance or getting his friend from next door, the bar owner, to help. It seemed as if we ought to at least do something.

Finally, Grandma took me by the arm and led me out of the room, leaving him there to sleep off the high.

Grandma White was a strong woman, a typical southern lady. She cooked and tended to housecleaning daily. Typically good-natured and eager to lend a helping hand, Grandma was easy to be around. Her piercing crystal blue eyes looked right into you, in a reassuring way that let you know she *saw* you—that you mattered.

It was hard understanding why she and Dad couldn't get along. When Uncle David was over—and my father was gone to sea—things seemed normal. Uncle David and Grandma got along just fine most of the time, as regular as any folks. If my father were there, though, things got heated just as they always did, and Uncle David would join right in.

Uncle David wasn't there the day I thought my Daddy had died, nor was Lester Case, just me and Grandma. I suppose Grandma did her best to make me feel better, though I don't recall much after the incident, just that I was scared out of my mind to see him sprawled out that way, shaking, lost to whatever force had dragged him under, had shaken his body and soul. I'd figure out later, most likely, he'd overdosed on that day. Luckily, it hadn't killed him.

That afternoon it became clear to me how important the drugs were to him, so important he'd risk his health, his life even. So important that an afternoon passed out on a recliner in a drug-induced stupor held precedence over spending time with his son and mother. The world opened up to me a little further that day, and I witnessed in it an ugliness I'll never forget, a demonic evilness called *addiction*. That day also served as a warning: this is the horror of substance abuse. But, addiction is cunning and baffling and, unfortunately, it was a warning I wouldn't heed.

Without a family, man, alone in the
world, trembles with the cold.
ANDRE MAUROIS

CHAPTER 3
Fitting In

I
F LIVING WITH GRANDMA WAS DIFFICULT WHEN MY
father was there, living with my mother offered no better comfort. Grandma's house had the security and warmth I found in her loving care. My mother's house had church.

Of course, there were other benefits to being at Mom's house besides singing gospel songs and Sunday school. My brothers were there, and at Mom's house, I could watch TV. Grandma White wasn't much for television, though there were the movies when Grandma would do her weekly shopping. But, Mom had a television I could watch anytime I wanted, and my brothers and I would play outside. Pete and Terry were so much older than me that they were past the point of wanting—or being willing—to play ball or tag or "cops and robbers" with their baby brother. Billy and Mark, though, were closer in age to me.

Because I didn't spend any significant time around my mother and brothers until around the age of six, except for the occasional day here and there—and church when I was lucky enough to be there on a Sunday— the whole situation felt strange and foreign. Grandma White felt more like my mother than my actual mother did. I remember the first few times I stayed with them for several days in a row; I felt awkward and didn't know quite what to do with myself. It was like going to play at someone else's house, someone you didn't know well.

It seemed to me that my brothers also felt strange around me, as if they were wondering who this kid was that they hardly knew. That feeling—the extreme sense of feeling out of place—didn't last forever, but it never completely went away.

Of all of them, Billy was my favorite. Though Mark was closer in age to me, he kept more to himself, often spending hours alone in his bedroom. As we got older, I hung out with Billy the most, sometimes the two of us getting into trouble. This isn't to say that I wouldn't have wanted a close relationship with Pete, Terry, and Mark. More than anything—except for my father to be calm and kind—I wished for a connection with my other family, my mother and brothers. What's the old saying, . . . "Wish in one hand, spit in the other"?

See which one fills up faster.

Holidays, especially, seemed to mark the divide between me and my mother's other sons and her family. Grandma White went out of her way to make sure I took part in holidays at my mother's house. She'd see to the arrangements, and though she didn't drive, she'd always make sure I had a way to and from my mother's. Holidays didn't happen at Grandma White's house. There was never Thanksgiving dinner or presents around a Christmas tree with Grandma and Daddy, so she made sure that I got a proper holiday. What she never knew was how unconnected I felt to all the festivities happening with my mother's family or, even, their everyday life. I can't really remember a time with my mother's family when I felt like one of them, that I fit in.

I remember a Thanksgiving with my mother and brothers and my maternal grandparents. I had to be six or seven. Mom's parents had moved out to Marietta, within the Duval County limits but on the other side of the St. Johns River. Grandma Taylor, especially, never seemed to show much emotion for me, though she was close to Pete and Terry and somewhat to Billy and Mark.

On this particular Thanksgiving Day, I'd done something wrong in Grandma Taylor's opinion. I've no recall of what offense I'd committed, but I remember my grandmother grabbing hold of me by my hair and pulling me into the living room to my mother. As far as I know, I never saw her act that way toward the other boys, only to me.

Granddaddy Carl, my mother's stepfather, was nicer, but I found it difficult to form a relationship with Grandma Taylor. I made it a point to be quiet around her and stay out of her sight. At times, I was so uncomfortable around her that I'd never do even the most normal of kid things, such as go inside her refrigerator for a soda or enter her house without knocking first.

I don't know what my mother said or did when Grandma Taylor pulled me by my hair that Thanksgiving afternoon. My mother wasn't the type to be combative or get riled up about what was going on around her. She always had her hands so busy taking care of the other boys that whatever I had going on would just have to wait. I don't blame my mother, though, for my feeling so disconnected from her and her family. She had a hard life and her circumstances were such that she was doing the best she could.

My mother tried to explain to me on several occasions that the reason she'd signed over custody of me to my father had to do with the fact that she had Rh-negative blood, a dangerous condition for pregnant women and their babies. More specifically, while she was pregnant with her sixth son, Joel—who's eight years younger than I am and born from her fourth marriage—she'd been told by hospital staff that she'd need to give my father custody in case she died during childbirth. She signed over legal custody of me to my father at that time.

After Mom delivered Joel, she tried to get my father to reassign custody back to her, but he refused. While it wasn't lost on me that the legal custody issue didn't account for the nature of my living arrangements before the age of eight, I chose to accept my mother's account of things and tried to understand the situation from her point of view, which wasn't easy at times.

At six, I went to the first grade. I hadn't gone to kindergarten, and I remember feeling worried about what school would be like. Would it be another place where I wouldn't feel comfortable? Or, would it be like church and I'd want to be there all the time?

It wouldn't be like church.

When I was six years old, my father moved Grandma and me from the two-story house downtown on 8th Street to an area of town southeast of the St. Johns River, within the larger community of Arlington. According to the map, this Jacksonville neighborhood was named Woodland Acres; according to the police, the rough streets were known as Sin City.

Sin City was full of dysfunctional families such as my own. No one seemed to have any money around the neighborhood. Drugs and alcohol were everywhere. I remember that most of the kids I played with came from broken homes. It was rare to see a home with a mom and dad and kids, what I considered a "normal" life. Of course, I didn't come from a normal life myself, so even though the place was chaotic and not always the safest place to be, I felt a kinship with the people there. I got where they were coming from.

I attended Woodland Acres Elementary, square in the middle of Sin City. Right away, school felt difficult. Another foreign place—like my mother's house. My first grade teacher was Mrs. Perkins, and she was nice but always expected the children to know a lot. I was never one to raise my hand and ask for help if I didn't know something. I'd rather sit and wait for recess or for the day to end so I could walk home from school and play with the other kids in the neighborhood.

On the first few days of school, Mrs. Perkins asked us to take out our pencils and sheets of paper, the elementary-ruled kind with the three wide lines. We were to write the alphabet as best we could, to see how much we remembered from kindergarten and to practice our handwriting.

I didn't know the alphabet. No one had ever taken the time to teach me my letters or numbers. I was coming into the first grade with nothing. I sat silently and stared at the empty sheet of elementary-ruled paper, watching as the other kids carefully wrote the alphabet letter by letter.

I suppose from the first days, I felt like school would not be a place I'd find success. I suppose I could have raised my hand and asked Mrs. Perkins for help or taken my blank sheet of paper home and asked Grandma to teach me the alphabet, but I didn't do either of those things. I'd learn to read and write eventually, but school and I didn't hit it off from the start.

It wasn't long before getting in trouble at school was a daily occurrence. My nickname at Woodland Acres was "Redneck Bully Boy," a name I earned after beating up several boys in the first grade. I wasn't doing much reading or mathematics in elementary school, but I did find two subjects I excelled in: getting in fights and kissing the girls.

I loved being a tough guy on the playground, bullying the weaker boys. At times, I'd take on boys bigger than me. Sometimes I'd get "swats," what the principal and teachers called corporal punishment. When I wasn't finding a fight, I was trying to kiss girls down in the culverts behind the school building.

Grandma, nor my dad, ever came to school that I remember, even when I would get swats or be called down to the principal's office. Parent-Teacher Night came and went without a visit from little Timmy White's family. Education and school just weren't things that held any importance in my family. Someone—Grandma, I suppose—signed me up for school, so I showed up, walking the mile there and then back.

When second grade came, my father enrolled me in Trinity Baptist. It was the late sixties, and in Jacksonville forced busing was in effect. I know for a fact that the reason I went to Trinity Baptist School was because Dad didn't want me going to school with black students. He'd done everything so far that he thought was right: married my mother so I'd have his last name, paid Grandma to raise me, and now he was going to enroll me in a Christian school to keep me from having to be around black folks. He made no secret of why I had to change schools, and I was too young to comprehend the blatantly racist sentiment. Had I understood, I was still much too afraid of him to object.

Second grade meant a new school, more unfamiliar surroundings. It also meant the first time I'd go live with complete strangers.

As with why I only went to my mother's house sometimes and didn't live with her and my brothers, why I went to live with the family who owned the buses that transported students to Trinity Baptist School was a mystery to me. I didn't know the guy who owned the buses or his family for anything, not more than any random stranger on the street.

I knew Grandma had taken ill, though. Taking care of a little boy drained the energy from her tired bones. She was strong, but even a strong person has limits. Though Grandma needed a break and time to recoup, why I ended up with the bus company family beat the heck out of me.

I suppose they needed the money.

I never watched money change hands, but I got the general impression from what was said that my father paid the man a good price to board and feed me. Turned out it was a good deal for the man all around, as he also got free labor.

The man's wife and three kids were nice enough to me. But him? I don't think he knew the definition of nice—or of compassion. I became a work animal, tending to the house and yard chores without so much of a mention of thanks or kind words to a little kid whose dad had dropped him off with a small bag of clothes and not much else.

One time in particular stands out. The man wanted a fire pit dug in the backyard, and he saw to it that I was going to be the one to dig it.

The space he marked out was eight by eight feet and three feet deep—back-breaking work for a seven year old. Sweat dripped off my face under the searing Florida sun. I shoveled dirt as fast as I could, while he stood over me, yelling to shovel faster.

The man's voice had a quality to it, a tone that told me he was having fun watching me sweat.

"Boy, you as slow as turtles running uphill in molasses," he said.

I knew better than to come back at him. Head down and mouth shut, I kept shoveling until the fire pit was dug. That night, every muscle in my weary body ached.

I stayed with the bus company family most of second grade, until I went to live with my mother and brothers. Why that arrangement wasn't made earlier was another mystery to me.

Life, and how things played out, rarely made sense to me. One day I was with my grandma; then I was with the bus company family; then I was with my mother. No one stopped to sit me down and explain circumstances to me. Perhaps my ability to process and understand change—and to cope with life's difficulties—would have been better, easier, if only someone had taken the initiative.

I knew my father tried to do his best by me. I mean, it wasn't as if he threw up his hands and said, *Hell, we ain't got any use for the little fella.* No one pinned a note to my shirt and left me on the church steps. My father tried to ensure I was fed and taken care of—even if he had to pay strangers to see to it.

But I always got the impression that my needs came second—maybe third or fourth even—to what he had going on, which was mainly the Merchant Marines and his addiction. If taking care of me didn't mean having to give up what he wanted to do, then things could be okay. Plain and simple, I was an accident, and what to do with me was beginning to be a recurring problem. I was only seven but could tell that I didn't fit in anywhere really, except with Grandma, whose health was failing. Already, life was a series of confusing moves and shuffling from one house to another, one unfamiliar and strange environment to the next.

Life was only about to get worse.

What we desire our children to become,
we must endeavor to be before them.

CHAPTER 4

Chaos and Confusion

T HE DAY STARTED CALM—AS CALM AS ANY DAY COULD
with a father whose mood could flip in an instant. Calm become rage;
rage become violence.

Dad had picked me up from the bus company family's house after
a phone call, during which I'd pleaded to come home, finally insisting.
I'd had enough of digging holes. For a while, I lived with my mother
and brothers, until I ended up back with Dad and Grandma. Grandma
seemed to be feeling better, but I could tell things were hard on her. Her
health had deteriorated.

This particular day Dad was home from sea. I don't remember where
we were headed or why we were going, but for some reason Dad got a
notion to drive down Heckscher Drive, headed north. We made it as far
as Sister's Creek before all hell broke loose.

Sister's Creek runs from the intersection of the St. Johns River to where
Fort George River joins the Intracoastal Waterway. The drawbridge that
spans the creek is a favorite spot of local fishers, mostly regular folks
fishing for fun or, which is often the case, for dinner. The bridge is a
good spot for catching red drum and trout. Folks line along the bridge's
span with their spinning rods and five-gallon buckets. I would watch the
fishers in anticipation when we'd drive across a bridge, hoping one might

reel in a catch just as we drove past, which was the case on that afternoon.

It must have been late spring or early summer. I remember enjoying the nice weather and the clear azure sky, watching in amazement as the fish the man had fresh on his line flopped back and forth, fighting to break free. We'd pulled a short ways onto the bridge when Dad stopped to give me a better look at the fisherman's catch. It looked like a trout of some sort, maybe a yellowmouth or a speck, about a good fifteen inches in length, just big enough to be a legal catch and a decent-sized supper.

Cars zipped past us on the opposite lane of the bridge. Dad's old Rambler had seen major wear and tear, and getting the window cranked down took a bit of effort. Seemingly in a good mood, Dad laughed as I fought with the window crank.

The window finally down, I called out, "Let me see! Show her this way." From behind us, the blast of a horn shattered the moment. Turning my head to look back at who was honking, I heard my father cuss and sensed him reach across the car. Quickly, I turned back to my father as he reached toward the Rambler's glove box, which was broken and tied up by a wire clothes hanger.

The muscles in my father's red face and neck stretched tight, his jaw clenched. Something in him had snapped, exploding him into a place of fury and mania. He struggled to open the glove box and, in the process, gashed the top of his right hand. Instantly, blood spurt in all directions, splattering against the dashboard, against me, and all down my father's arm. Instantly, I knew why he was reaching over, what he was madly searching for in his fit of rage. In the glove compartment lay Dad's gun. He had slashed his hand reaching for his 38-caliber pistol.

They say time slows down in moments of great emotional impact. The event on Sister's Creek Bridge couldn't have occurred in more than a few minutes, but it felt longer, not played out in some overly dramatized slow motion but sensed second by second, crystallized—the scene seared into my brain.

I watched wide-eyed in horror as Dad, cursing, leaped from the car and ran to the black man behind the wheel of a blue Ford pickup truck. The man had been unfortunate to have had his window down. As fast as my father made it to his truck, the unlucky guy hadn't time to roll up his window. Or, perhaps, he'd been too shocked to move—witnessing this lunatic jump from an old sedan, hand and arm covered in blood, charging at him, pistol drawn, like some savage animal ready to kill.

Of course, I was too afraid to do anything but watch from the front seat of Dad's Rambler. There was no way I was going anywhere, even jumping out the car to ask the fishermen for help wasn't a thought that crossed my mind. I'd learned long ago that the best thing to do when Dad got like this was stay as quiet and still as possible. I did turn in my seat, though, to follow what happened.

My father had his pistol right to the man's head, threatening to pull the trigger. With the windows down, I could hear the man begging for his life.

"Please don't kill me, mister," he cried. "Please don't kill me!"

The man's face twisted in an expression of fear and horror. I wanted to help him. Though I was only eight, I understood that feeling and knew he believed, truly believed, in that moment he was going to die. He was going to be shot in the head by a crazed man on a drawbridge in northeast Florida because he dared to honk his horn at the wrong guy at the wrong time.

I watched as my father held the gun to the man's head and screamed, "I'm gonna kill you!"

The man got quiet and shut his eyes. Maybe out of plumb fear or maybe having given up, resigned himself to the fact of his imminent death, he went silent. For whatever reason he did it, when the man stopped begging, my father drew back his pistol and moved back toward the Rambler.

Immediately, I turned in my seat and stared forward out the front window and to the drawbridge beyond. I didn't look at the fishermen to my right or at my father as he entered the car. Still cursing, he sat down, placing the pistol between us on the car seat.

I held my breath as my father reached over to the back seat and grabbed a shirt he happened to have in the car. He tied the shirt around the gash on his hand and said, "Man can't even stop to show his son a fish." Then he drove off, as if nothing more than a minor irritation had occurred.

As we made it over the other side of the bridge, I caught a glimpse in the rearview mirror at the road behind us. The man had made it to the other side of the bridge. Once on the other end, he'd pulled his truck off the side of the road and onto the grass. I couldn't see his face any longer as we pulled away from him. Silently, I hoped he was okay. I told myself he probably just needed a few minutes to pull himself together. I sure would have.

My father seemed fine now. The rage had passed. Things were as they had been, and we would never speak of that moment. Not then. Not ever.

An event like that changes a person—writes on his or her subconscious in a way that can never be erased or scratched out or rewritten. A moment like that plays out the same way, over and over, like a broken record. Funny though, it's only now as I consider the events, in order to permanently record them, that I wonder what the fishermen on the bridge thought. What did they do and say and think? Why didn't they stop my father? Fear of being shot themselves, I suppose.

Often, with events involving my father, I could step out from the situation, detach myself, almost as if I were watching a movie, wild things happening to someone else. But that day on Sister's Creek burned so deeply, so instantaneously, I'd no chance to separate myself from it.

I'd get another horrific moment on a bridge, on another day alone with my father. On that day, I'd come even closer to death—and that time, my own.

MY FATHER'S INSANITY AND INSTABILITY PLAYED OUT IN OTHER ways during this time of my life. Dad loved camping. When I was around the age of eight to the age of eleven, Dad bought a series of converted campers, vans, and minibuses, even an old bread truck, and got into camping in the woods. He particularly liked driving out to Florida's panhandle or up to the Okefenokee Swamp on the Florida-Georgia border.

Sometimes, Dad would bring a friend along on our camping trips, which was good because it shifted my father's attention from me to the other person. When someone else traveled along, things were mostly okay, but when we were alone together, the trip almost always went badly, beginning with when he'd drink or get high.

Dad's habit of flying off the handle at any little thing would sometimes mean that I might be dragged from my bed late at night. Immediately, a sense of doom would fall over me.

Dad would barge into my bedroom and rouse me from sleep. "Timothy! Come on son, we're getting out of here. I can't take this shit no more."

I'd get dressed as quickly as I could. When he got the mind to leave, there wasn't time for packing an overnight bag.

He'd stomp about, ranting and raving that Grandma was getting too much for him. "Your Grandma's killing me, son. She's killing me!"

Then, we'd load into whatever makeshift camper he had at the time and drive like a Nascar racer over to the panhandle or up to the Okefenokee. Once arrived, he'd park in the woods, ranting all through night about how fed up he was with it all, how he couldn't take it anymore.

None of it made any sense to me: the yelling, his tantrums, running off in the middle of the night. Sometimes we'd stay in the woods for days, Dad with his guns, drinking and carrying on about one thing, then the other. Eventually, he'd get tired of being in the woods or run out of alcohol and drugs, and we'd drive back to Grandma's.

THOUGH THERE CERTAINLY WEREN'T AS MANY GOOD TIMES with my father as I would have liked, there were calmer times, times when Dad and I would connect. These rare occasions usually involved trips away from Jacksonville.

In one way or another, my father's life always seemed under duress, whether self-imposed or brought on by his own dysfunctional choices. My father was in battle with the world on a daily basis. Every day was a day of tension. The one place he genuinely seemed to relax was when he left the city and all that his life there entailed. I suppose that might be why he joined the Merchant Marines in the first place, to get away.

Our trips together, the good ones at least, usually revolved around fishing. Unlike the nightmare midnight "camping trips," our fishing trips were generally peaceful. Dad's psychological instability appeared less extreme when we'd go down to Cedar Key on Florida's Gulf Coast. The blue waters of the Gulf provided plenty of good fishing.

We'd always stay at the same little hotel right near the fishing pier. An old man and lady, whom Daddy had known for years, owned the hotel. I remember the old lady. Wearing a floppy, wide-brimmed hat, she pulled her fishing cart behind her and fished off the side of a small wood bridge, right next to the bigger, new bridge. We'd get up around 5:00 A.M. and get to the bridge just as the sun was coming up. We'd spend all morning and much of the afternoon fishing off the small bridge.

I remember once when I was seven or eight how Daddy had gotten me a new rod and reel. I sat on the bridge with my new fishing rod, proud that I had a shiny new rod all my own. As I enjoyed the feeling, a fish came along and latched onto the hook, yanking the rod right out of my hands. I panicked. I was sure I'd be in trouble for losing the new rod. Daddy had just bought it for me, and he didn't buy me much. Whatever it was on that hook, it came along and grabbed hold of that rod as swift as an arrow. I guess I didn't have a good hold on it.

Daddy didn't get mad about it. Though he still drank, he was calm during those times. Times like those, I'd catch a glimpse of the father I knew was behind his mask of anger, resentment, and substance abuse.

Seeing that side of my father made this period all the more chaotic and confusing. Why couldn't he be this way, as he was on our fishing trips, all the time? What was it that drove him to abuse drugs and alcohol, and how did that abuse influence his thoughts and behavior? Of course, I was too young to have those answers, to understand the destructive nature of using substances to cope with life's stresses.

MY ANGER AND RESENTMENT GREW WITH EACH OF MY father's outbursts and rounds of violent behavior. Though he didn't strike out at me physically, the emotional blows he landed would eventually pound away any good feelings I held for him and made me distance myself from others, especially grownups, with the exception of Grandma White.

My father was not the only one, though, who continued to disappoint me and for whom my anger and resentment increased year by year. My mother—as it felt to me at the time—seemed unconcerned with my life and made only half-hearted attempts to involve me in hers. When I was around her and my brothers, it sometimes seemed to me that she cared for and loved me, but when I was not there, I wondered if she thought of me at all.

As an adult and parent myself, I can look back now and rationalize that she must have done the best she could in the situation and with the resources available to her, but as a child, it didn't feel that way. I had no real understanding of what was going on, and, in the absence of any adult's explanation of the situation, I filled in the missing pieces on my own. My mother didn't care. That's how I saw it then. It isn't easy now to say so or to put to ink and paper, but that was the reality of my thinking at the time.

Given my perception, as I grew older, I began to build up a wall to my mother, separating myself even further from her and my "other" life with her, my brothers, and all the relatives on her side of my so-called family. It didn't feel much like family or what, in my young mind, I imagined family to be. Times around her and my brothers were still awkward, though they'd gotten somewhat more comfortable over the years, and I looked forward to the few times a year when I knew I'd spend time with Mom and things had a hope of being good. One of those times was on my birthday.

Every year on my birthday, Mom would take me to the Ringling Brothers Circus, which always came to Jacksonville around the first week of February. It was our tradition. Sometimes one or more of my brothers would come along, but I thought of it as my time with Mom, the two of us. I began looking forward to the day weeks in advance, talking to Grandma about it, telling my friends how I was going to the circus, how much fun it would be and what I'd do there. It was a small thing, but it was something. In my life so far, I'd learned how to make the best of small things.

I was nearing my tenth birthday, and the circus was in town. The days leading up to my birthday, I thought of little else than the precious time I'd have on my special day—my mother's attention focused on me. Already, I could smell fresh roasted peanuts and buttered popcorn and hear the trumpeting of the elephants and the roar of the crowd's applause.

Finally, the big day arrived. I got up early the morning of my birthday and waited for my mother to pick me up. Around noon, I started to worry. By one o'clock, I stared continually out the front window, leaving only to ask Grandma half a dozen times when my mother was coming to get me. Around two o'clock, Grandma made a phone call to my mother. I could hear her on the kitchen phone telling my mother, "He's your son and he's waiting on you." From the tone in Grandma's voice, I knew my mother wasn't coming. My heart sank with the realization that either she had forgotten my birthday or just didn't care enough to keep up our special tradition.

At the time, it never occurred to me that my mother might not have had the funds to take me to an event or put gas in her car to come get me. I didn't consider that maybe something had happened to get in her way, which may very well have been the case with four other boys at home and a newborn son. By that time, my mother had married for the fourth time and given birth to another boy, my younger brother Joel. I know now there were many understandable reasons why she didn't show that day, though she didn't offer any explanation that I remember. I do remember Grandma said something to me to the effect that my mother ought to "spend time with her kid" and something ungracious about my mother's character that I've long since forgotten or blocked out.

Hearing Grandma speak ill of my mother hurt but only solidified in my mind the idea that I was not wanted, did not fit in anywhere, and was not bound in some loving and meaningful way to my mother—and, by extension, to the rest of the world outside Grandma White's house. Life was a series of one chaotic and confusing event at a time, seemingly unconnected. I wanted to understand it but could make no sense of anything around me, other than my Grandma loved me and I felt safe with her.

I continued to build walls and strengthen the ones already erected. By ten years old, I'd firmly established in my mind that there wasn't a life for me that felt normal and fitting. I'm sure I didn't consider it so rationally or intentionally, but somewhere in my impressionable, immature mind, I decided I'd get what I could out of life. If anyone got in my way—well, too bad for them.

Be alert, stand firm in the faith,
be courageous, be strong.
1 CORINTHIANS 16:13

CHAPTER 5
Wedding Bells and Bullet Holes

W HEN I WAS ELEVEN, MY FATHER MARRIED CAROLYN
Donaldson. We moved out of Grandma's house and into Carolyn's
singlewide mobile home.

Dad had dated Carolyn a short while before she found herself pregnant.
The two got married right away. Dad and I moved our few belongings
to her trailer. The six of us squeezed into the cramped space: Carolyn,
Dad, her three children, and me. I knew Carolyn would soon regret the
marriage. She and my father hardly knew each other, and I was sure she'd
no clue what she'd gotten herself into. It was only a matter of time.

It wasn't long before my prediction came true.

From the beginning, life with Carolyn and her kids was a struggle.
Carolyn's previous husband had died in a fireworks factory explosion,
leaving her to raise three children. I suppose Dad's good looks and
charisma—an impressive combination when he was sober—appealed to
her. She was a nice woman, and I liked her. The kids were all right, though
the oldest girl, Vicki, didn't take to me well. I figured her father hadn't
been deceased long, and her mother had already remarried and moved in
the guy and his kid. I can't blame her for feeling some resentment. I wasn't
happy about being there myself.

Dad quit going out to sea and found a job working security at a nearby airfield. He'd no other skills besides those he acquired as a merchant seaman. I never saw him fix or construct anything, and he'd never finished high school, so job opportunities were limited. His deep, authoritative voice, intimidating facial expressions, and love of guns, though, suited him well for security guard work. He drove a golf car around Craig Municipal Airport and increased his drinking and drugging at home with Carolyn and us kids.

By this time, Dad had traded in heroin for prescription pills. He'd put down the needle but was heavy into the bottle—booze bottle *and* pill bottle—and smoked pot on a regular basis. Carolyn wasn't into drugs, but she drank tons of coffee and chain-smoked cigarettes. Between Dad and Carolyn's cigarette dependency, the trailer reeked of smoke. Soon, I found myself picking up the habit, surrounded by it and out of my Grandma's care. Carolyn and I would smoke cigarettes together, and she'd confide in me her unhappiness with Dad.

The midnight camping trips had stopped, but my father's anger and unpredictability grew even stronger. He spent hours in the trailer's backroom recording cassette tapes of strange talk, political rants. He'd package the tapes and send them to people who were part of some fringe political party he'd become affiliated with or to whomever he thought might listen and help him and his group change things in whatever way they thought needed changing. To me, all his ranting sounded like sheer craziness.

Sometimes, he'd take me with him downtown on Adams Street to the American Dixie Barber Shop, where he'd talk politics with the owner Warren Folks. I knew very little of Folks or his beliefs at the time but would learn later that Folks proclaimed himself leader of the local KKK and was an avid supporter of J. B. Stoner. Stoner was an American segregationist, founder of the National States' Rights Party, and convicted in 1980 of the 1958 bombing of the Bethel Baptist Church in Birmingham, Alabama. I've no knowledge of my father's involvement with Stoner or the National States' Rights Party, but I do know he considered Warren Folks a friend and that Folks was involved with certain KKK activity in Jacksonville at the time.

One night, soon after I turned twelve, my father took me into his and Carolyn's bedroom in the trailer. On the bed sat a white clothes box, large enough to pack a bulky coat or a wedding gown. He'd been drinking most of the day, and I could sense he wanted to tell me something, to share something important to him. I hadn't had many moments like this with my dad and wanted to see what was in the box.

Dad stood next the bed, the white box beside him. I stood at the foot of the bed, waiting quietly.

"Son, you're twelve years old now." His face stern and serious, he looked from me to the box, then back at me. "That makes you a man according to the Bible."

I had no idea what he was getting at, but hearing him call me "a man" made me pay even more attention.

Slowly, he lifted the top cover of the box to reveal what lay inside. From the foot of the bed, I couldn't see into the box. I stepped to the side and up a few feet, craning my neck a bit to spy what lay inside.

Carefully, he removed the item from the box. The long sleeves unfolded as he held the item up to shoulder height in front of him. The long, full purple robe fell almost to his feet. I stared at the red patch with its white cross. My father held the robe up to himself, the patch against his heart.

"I'm showing this to you, son, because you're a man now." His eyes beamed with pride, intensely locked on mine. "One day, you'll make up your own mind about things. Right now, I'm showing you this, so you know what your old man's about."

I didn't know what to say. Better, I figured, to say nothing than risk saying the wrong thing.

"This robe here makes me a leader," he continued. The robe's deep purple color made my father's green eyes sparkle even brighter.

I could hear in his voice the pride he felt at this accomplishment, leader in the Jacksonville Ku Klux Klan. I'd no desire to hear more and waited quietly as he folded the robe and put it back into its box. The moment I'd been eager to experience was over. It made a lasting impression on me, as he'd intended, but not for the reasons he'd wanted.

I had seen Dad act kindly to many people, black and white, and especially to the elderly, but I'd never really considered his feelings about racial issues. I was twelve and such things didn't concern me much. There had been the incident on Sister's Creek Bridge, but I'd always figured his violent reaction had more to do with his own short temper than anything racially motivated.

I didn't know what his exact activities in the Klan were or how his crazy political recordings related and never asked, but I knew he was getting worse. I had no interest in finding out more about either one or being a part of any of it. I spent as much time as I could away from him and as an ally to Carolyn, helping her devise a plan as to what to do should Dad become violent or dangerous. Increasingly, he drank more and popped all kinds of pills: valium, quaaludes, various opiates. As Carolyn's pregnancy advanced, Dad's behavior became even more erratic and dangerous.

Perhaps as justification of his drug use, Dad would hold up a bottle of prescription pills and say, "Son, this is medicine. This is medicine I've got to take."

Constantly doctor shopping, my father always had pills on him and stayed high most of the time. I never saw him shoot up with heroin, but I watched him down pills on many occasions. Valiums were his favorites. When he wanted to catch a stronger buzz, he'd take quaaludes or some opioid.

At some point, he may have gone to a doctor to get off heroin and been prescribed methadone, or a similar drug, to wean off the dope, but clearly that period had passed and now he was just a full-on pill head. I knew he was hooked on the drugs and that they weren't "medicine," at least in the way he wanted me to believe. I couldn't tell if it was guilt or shame or some misguided sense of parental duty that made him offer up an explanation, but it didn't matter—the effect was the same. Watching him drunk and high only caused me to resent him more and drove a larger wedge between us.

He wasn't fooling anyone, especially me.

I'm sure as Carolyn's pregnancy advanced, she wanted even more for Dad to get off the drugs and stop drinking. Things were tense enough around the trailer without adding a newborn into the mix. Dad's frequent outbursts scared her. Already a quiet, nervous woman, the short time with my father was beginning to show on her, physically and in her behavior. Frown lines seemed burrowed into her face, and her eyes appeared to dull a bit more with each passing day.

I felt bad for her. She'd always been kind to me and deserved a better husband and father to her child than my father. Carolyn and I would sit at the small kitchen table, smoking cigarettes, and plan what to do if things got too out of hand. I told her the best thing to do was just leave—and as quickly as possible. She was eight months pregnant when that dreaded moment came.

Carolyn's belly popped out from her skinny frame big and round like an oversized basketball. Dad had been drinking all night and was in a foul mood. Combining pills with alcohol escalated his violent tendencies, and I began to worry when he downed beer after beer. I tried to get the other kids to stay out of his way, but they didn't have as much experience as I did with tiptoeing around when he was in one of his moods.

I don't know exactly what it was that set off my father on this particular night. One of Carolyn's kids—perhaps Vicki, who was my age and never took to my father—may have said something he considered "back talk." We were all in the trailer's front room, the living room area, when Dad lost it and pulled out the 38-pistol he kept on himself at all times.

Before we could duck or run from the room, Dad fired a bullet into the trailer wall. Even in his crazed state, I could tell he wasn't trying to kill us, just get our attention real good and assert his absolute authority. Carolyn and her kids looked terrified. Oddly, I remained calm.

I yelled at Carolyn and the kids to get out of the trailer, and we all ran to the back door. We rarely used the back door, which had no stairs, a four-foot drop. I could hear my father coming up behind us, cursing and threatening to kill us all. There was no time to waste.

I made the other kids go first. Next, I jumped to the hard ground, then held out my hand to help Carolyn.

Every second counted. Dad hadn't fired at us in the trailer, aiming instead at the wall. I couldn't guarantee, though, that he wouldn't change his mind and correct his aim, seeing as we'd run from him, a clear violation of his control over us.

Awkwardly, Carolyn grabbed hold my hand and jumped. Luckily, she landed on both feet.

Darkness enveloped us.

As we ran into the night, I shouted, "I knew this would happen!"

I heard my father swearing from the trailer's back door but didn't turn to watch him. We made it away from the trailer and out of the neighborhood as quickly as possible. I suppose we stayed with Carolyn's mother for the night. How we got there or how long we remained gone from my father, I don't remember.

It wasn't too long after that when the baby came—stillborn and with its umbilical cord wrapped around its neck. The doctors thought the cord might have shifted around the baby's neck when Carolyn jumped down from the back door that night. To my knowledge, no one ever told my father the explanation offered by the doctors—for fear of what he might do.

I know I didn't dare tell him.

Shortly after the baby's delivery, Dad bought a house in Hortense, Georgia, with the idea that we'd all move there at the end of the school year. He'd enrolled me into University Christian School at the beginning of sixth grade, another church school meant to keep me segregated from black students. My defiant behavior kept me in trouble, and I often skipped classes. I kept cigarettes on me that I'd bummed from Carolyn or outright stolen from somewhere. I made no attempt to hide my smoking habit.

Toward the last quarter of school, some kid—just a pansy tattletale as far as I was concerned—threatened to tell on me for carrying cigarettes. I don't know where he caught me smoking. I might have even lit up right in the school hallway. I wanted others to witness my attitude and anger, though the thought of my father finding out about my getting in any serious trouble terrified me. This kid was going to tell on me for something sure to get me at least suspended, if not worse.

We were alone in the hallway, just the tattletale and me. Before he could finish threatening to turn me in, I pulled out my pocketknife and shoved him against the nearest wall. I'd taken to bringing the knife to school about the same time I started toting smokes. Both, I thought, made me a tough guy, not to be messed with. It was just a small blade but big enough to scare the heck out of a sixth-grade snitch.

I was sort of savoring the look of fear on the kid's face when a teacher rounded the corner of the hallway and caught me in the act, my knife to the kid's throat.

That was my last day at University Christian.

Dad was furious—more, I think, over the fact that he'd paid for the whole year in advance and stood losing a good chunk of money. There were no refunds for expulsion.

After UC expelled me, we left Jacksonville for Hortense, earlier than expected. Carolyn's first husband's family lived in Georgia. Though her mother lived in Jacksonville, she didn't mind the idea of being closer to her children's relatives. Dad went back to the Merchant Marines; gone for one month out to sea, then back for one month.

I finished out sixth grade in Hortense and spent even more time helping Carolyn plot her escape from my father. The plan was that I'd leave with them, live with them wherever they went. I liked Carolyn, and things with my stepsisters and stepbrother were getting better. I didn't hear from Mom much. I talked on the phone to Grandma White sometimes, but she seemed fine without me around to worry over. Maybe I'd found a family I could fit into, feel good about.

I think it was less than five months in Hortense before Carolyn and her kids split. Funny, I don't remember anyone making a big production about them leaving. One day they were there. The next, they were gone.

Now, I was alone with my father.

Behavior is a mirror in which every one
displays his own image.
JOHANN WOLFGANG VON GOETHE

CHAPTER 6

Junior Criminal

L IVING WITH DAD IN GEORGIA COULDN'T LAST LONG. Having gone out to sea to work, my father needed a place to keep me. Soon after Carolyn and the kids left, Dad got on the phone, and I ended back in Jacksonville with my mother.

Mom lived in an apartment in Jacksonville's Westside. Pete and Terry lived with Grandma Taylor, but Mark, Billy, Joel, and I kept Mom's hands full. Born during her fourth marriage, which by now had already ended, four-year-old Joel demanded lots of attention. Mark was quiet and kept to himself. Out of the three older boys, I caused Mom the most grief. Billy, however, did his fair share of misbehaving and acting out, on occasion showing me how to have a "good time," such as the time he introduced me to shot-gunning beer.

The confusion I felt as a child had shifted to anger. My rebelliousness and defiance played out on a daily basis and in every aspect of my life. I was glad to be around Mom and my brothers, but I felt no solid connection to them. In fact, I didn't feel much of anything really—a callousness having developed over my heart, mind, and spirit. I wasn't overly aggressive, but I didn't care about anything or anyone, either. I wasn't mean to my mother, but I had no regard for rules or boundaries, not that there were many. Smoking, drinking, cutting school were all ways I could express my contempt for authority.

I remember the first day of seventh grade, standing apart from the other kids dressed in their first-day-of-school outfits, smoking a cigarette while we waited for the school bus. When the teachers issued textbooks the first day, I threw mine away. If the dopes at school were dumb enough to issue replacement books, I'd throw those away, too. I was determined to show anyone and everyone that I didn't give a lick about them, their rules, or their agendas. Not that I had a plan of my own; I didn't—but no one else's plan could bind me or dictate my actions. No, sir.

As soon as seventh grade started, I found a pack of running buddies. Boys made of the same cloth as me, from broken homes and lacking discipline, with no plans of their own. We skipped school and ran the streets, getting into all sorts of trouble.

Our typical school day consisted of getting on the bus to James Weldon Johnson, at that time a seventh-grade center, and walking back home. The school was over ten miles away, and the walk back to the apartments took all day. We didn't care. We weren't attending classes and had nothing else to do. Walking back home meant cutting through neighborhoods tougher than our own, but we weren't scared, even after thugs hassled us, demanding we hand over the little money in our pockets.

After a while of making the long trek from school to home, we took the opportunity to steal from convenience stores along the way. Sometimes the clerk behind the counter paid more attention when a pack of boys entered the store all at once, but often they didn't. We slipped merchandise into our pockets, quick and slick. Sometimes, we entered two at a time; one guy distracted the clerk while the other stole packs of cigarettes or food or alcohol, whatever we wanted and could fit in our jackets, pockets, or down our pants. Ripping off smokes helped me feed my nicotine habit. Soon into the school year, I developed another habit.

I'd seen kids smoke pot and wanted to try it but worried about what it would be like. Steve, my best buddy then, introduced me to weed. Getting high made me feel funny and mellow. I was over my worry after the first time. Steve and I got high and laughed our fool heads off. It wasn't long before I started getting high as often as I could. Along with my rebellion, I developed a bad case of the *don't-give-a-shits*. Nothing seemed important. Not only did I have no plan for anything in life, I had no desire to find one.

One good thing I did during this time, though, was begin thinking like an entrepreneur. I collected bottles for the five cents deposit, scouring trailer parks and asking folks if I could collect the empty bottles from under their trailers. I gave them three cents a bottle, then turned them in and pocketed the two-cent difference. Mostly, my brothers and I collected bottles for food money. I'd round up enough bottles to buy myself a combo special at Dairy Queen: a cheeseburger, Coke, and banana split. Money was super tight at home and going hungry a daily concern.

Smoking pot didn't keep me from collecting bottles, though, or bumming dimes at the Lil' Champ, which was another way I pocketed easy money, a skill I'd perfected with my father in the bar on 8th Street. I hung out near the phone booth, and when a grownup came along, I made a big production about needing money to call my mom. Grownups were easy to scam, real sympathetic to a little kid with big, sad eyes and a sob story.

Drinking and smoking wasn't going to stop me from doing what little I had going on, but when Steve and I got high, I wanted to feel that way all the time. I felt better about things, evened-out a bit. I didn't think much about it at the time, but I was using alcohol and drugs to cope with my life. I'd watched my father's drinking and drugging and hated it, but that didn't help me make the connection that maybe it wasn't a good thing for me.

Life amped up a level when I met John, whose mother managed the apartments where we lived. John ran wild like us boys and had no problem "borrowing" his mom's apartment master key. John, Steve, our buddy Erik, and I began stealing from apartment units in the complex. We broke into units during the day, when folks were at work and we were supposed to be in school.

Billy and Mark didn't participate in our robberies, and I kept my mouth shut about our criminal activities. I didn't feel bad about what I was doing; not telling my brothers wasn't a matter of guilt or shame. I didn't want to get caught. Billy got into his share of mischief. He drank beers sometimes, and he and his best friend Gary, who came to stay with us around that time and didn't leave for years, scammed restaurants out of meals and other petty kid stuff. I, on the other hand, stepped over a line: breaking into apartments was serious criminal behavior.

I took to it like a duck to water.

I had needs, and I was resourceful. Nothing was going to get in the way of what I wanted. The boys I ran with were just the same. We'd do whatever came to mind that seemed fun or got us what we wanted, regardless of the consequences, which we never really considered or talked about even. We never discussed what might happen if we got caught, how our parents would react, or what it might be like to get handcuffed and hauled off to juvenile detention.

I remember one trick we used to pull on the younger kids in the apartment. We'd get a couple of the nine- and ten-year-olds and us together for a poker game. I'd act like I didn't know how to play poker, which I did, and run them for their jars of change or birthday money. Some poor kid would hold up a straight, and I'd start fast-talking, telling them that a pair beat a straight or my clubs and spades beat out their full house. If one of the little kids put up a fuss or disagreed, I'd start talking faster, confusing them until they'd hand over their money.

We'd run the con on them all afternoon, until their pockets and change jars were empty, then laugh like hyenas at them behind their backs. Of course, I feel bad about it now, but at the time, as with anything else, I was wrapped in my own selfishness, thinking myself clever knowing how to manipulate people so easily.

It was clear to every one of the guys that I was the best at making up a lie on the spot or slinging a story that could get us out of trouble or score what we wanted. I had a talent for cock-and-bull stories and no problem dishing them out. But all the guys, in one way or another, were on a road that was no good. All of us had nothing to speak of and no plan for the future. For me, breaking into apartments, stealing from stores, and conning the clueless became a way to get my needs fulfilled—an easy and exciting way.

I didn't mind honest work, though mostly I had to do it alone. When I went out collecting bottles all day, my friends didn't want to go or wouldn't work as long and hard as I worked. I got the impression that maybe I had a stronger drive to get what I wanted, more so than them. They were fun to be around, but I could tell they weren't willing to work hard given the opportunity. I didn't mind walking for miles, walking sometimes all day, collecting enough bottles to have a few bucks in my pocket. I felt good about having been smart enough to earn money myself. Unfortunately, I felt even better when I was drunk or high.

Eventually, getting wasted became more important than being self-sufficient. It would become a need greater than fitting in, giving and receiving love, and finding direction. Soon, that need would take over everything.

Pain and foolishness lead to
great bliss and complete knowledge,
for Eternal Wisdom created nothing
under the sun in vain.
KHALIL GIBRAN

CHAPTER 7

Escape

I CAN STILL PICTURE IT: BILLY AND GARY TWIRLING BIG forks of spaghetti, steam rising from their plates, shoving pasta covered with thick tomato sauce into their mouths, stopping only to laugh or drink long swigs of sweet tea. From behind the restaurant's window, I couldn't smell it, but I imagined it smelled like the best spaghetti dinner in the world—garlic toast, a plateful of pasta, and fat Italian meatballs, a feast for the starving.

I was the starving.

Billy and his friend Gary wouldn't let me come into the restaurant with them. They'd run this scam before: order food, eat quickly, then go to the register all flustered and with some lie about having left their wallets at home. They'd make off out the door before the hostess or waitress could get a manager or call the cops. They'd done it dozens of times around the Westside, where there were enough Mom and Pop restaurants to do it a few dozen more. I didn't care that they got away with it so easily, what made me mad was that they never let me in on it.

As with everything else, I was an outsider looking in.

I watched my brother and his friend from outside the restaurant window and touched my belly when it grumbled. Why I couldn't be a part of their con baffled me. I could pull it off, probably better than them. More important, I wanted to be a part of what was going on in my brother's life—even if it was ripping off restaurants together.

However, I was the outsider and knew no way in. I couldn't understand why my life was such that I remained shut out of everything, or thought I was, at least. Why did other people have lives where they could walk into a restaurant and have a meal and I couldn't? How did I get handed this life, my life? What had I done wrong?

So many questions and no answers.

Running wild at James Weldon Johnson Seventh Grade Center, I got high when pot was available and drank when I could steal beer or convince someone to buy it for me. Being drunk or high made me tune out the questions spinning in my mind. I could escape from the world. By the end of seventh grade, I was an angry ball of energy and bravado, daring anyone to get in my way.

Remarkably, my teachers passed me from the seventh grade, probably just to get me out of the school. Eighth grade would mean attending Lake Shore Junior High, which was closer to our apartment—not that I had any intentions of making eighth grade any more successful than seventh had been.

My buddy Steve passed seventh grade, too, and went to Lake Shore with me. School bored and frustrated me, especially this one, and I made it a particular mission that year to raise holy hell from day one. I was constantly in trouble and no teacher or dean could tell me anything. The world had done me no favors, and I was going to make everyone pay for it.

Corporeal punishment was referred to as "getting swats." I can remember getting swats from the Eighth Grade Dean of Boys, who had one good arm, the other paralyzed. The dean would place a wooden school chair out in the hallway and command me to bend over. The whack of the paddle on my behind reverberated up and down the high-ceilinged hallway. I got swats on a weekly basis, and when I needed a break from school and wanted an excuse to stay home, I got suspended on purpose.

My list of offenses stretched down the school hallway, and teachers learned fast that whatever I was up to was no good. I skipped classes, smoked in the bathrooms, brought pot to school, mouthed off, and fought whoever was brazen enough to stand up to me.

Escape

At one point, the dean called the police to the school when my friend Tommy Harding and I went gone off campus with a girl, got high, and came back to school. The girl got caught stoned and told a school official who'd gotten her high. Once the police got involved, that was the beginning of the end at Lake Shore. Shortly after that incident, the dean and principal told my mother that something had to be done about me, insisting I be sent to a reformatory school or boys' home, someplace equipped to handle me.

Mom felt differently. She did her best to cope with the situation and talk some sense into me, but I was having none of it. Mostly, I wanted to escape. My acting out at school was probably a classic cry for attention, but what I remember feeling strongest at that time was an intense desire to be somewhere else. Anywhere else.

Drugs and alcohol provided that escape. Scoring either, however, wasn't always easy. Luckily, I had Steve—and Steve's mother.

Steve's mom liked Valium and had a big pill bottle full of it. Produced from the chemical diazepam, doctors prescribe Valium to treat anxiety, insomnia, and seizures, among other conditions. I don't know what of those conditions, if any, Steve's mom had, but Steve liked Valium just for chilling out. Little, yellow chill pills.

Unfortunately, I'd no idea how dangerous it could be to take a handful of chill pills.

It was Steve's big idea: pop his mom's Valium, then veg out at his apartment. The small pills looked like nothing, so I took a few, then a few more. In a short while, I began to feel dizzy and tired. The feeling—dramatic and overwhelming—surprised me. It was all I could do to stumble out of Steve's place and to our apartment, staggering through our front door, woozy and disoriented.

Billy was the first to see me in the drugged state. He pointed at me and yelled for Mom to come. "Come here! Tim's messed up." I dropped to the living room floor as I heard Billy yell, "Look at him! Tim's on drugs!"

And, I was—indeed. Drugged out of my mind and wanting only to fall asleep. I got up and stumbled to my bedroom while Billy continued to point out the obvious and Mom held onto me, keeping me from landing flat on my face in the middle of the hallway.

I slept, off and on, for two days. In retrospect, I don't imagine it was very wise to let me sleep it off, minus emergency room care. I guess my mother kept a close eye on me and could tell I'd be okay once the effects wore off. No one said much about the incident once I recovered, but my actions made the tension in the home greater, especially regarding what to do about me and my behavior. Even still, Mom had no intention of sending me to a boys' home and suggested often that I pray for guidance and the strength to behave myself.

I loved my mother, but I had a better idea.

Escape.

Around this period, I became more excited with the idea of escaping my life, often imagining what it might be like living somewhere else, on my own and free from the life around me. Thankfully—or at least I thought so then—I had my buddy Steve.

Steve had done something or other to upset his mom. Perhaps raiding her pill stash or stealing from her purse, who knows what? Whatever he'd done, Steve thought it would be a good idea to escape, too, and told me so. I was on the idea in a hot minute, adding to the notion by suggesting we run away to my dad's house in Hortense, Georgia. We could hitchhike our way up to Hortense and make ourselves a new life. Grow our hair long and live free.

Crazy thinking.

We took off to Hortense with only a few bucks between us and no plan for what we'd do once we got there. I remember a slight chill in the air when we left. Being shortsighted kids, we weren't bright enough to bring a heavy coat, much less supplies or camping gear or anything. We left in the morning, spending our little bit of money on the way for an order of fries and two Cokes, and made it almost to Hortense by nightfall. We'd been lucky to catch a few rides on the way.

A few miles from Dad's house, a policeman pulled alongside us and questioned what we were doing and where we were going.

I looked at Steve as if to tell him, *Play along.* "Evening, officer. We're going to my Dad's house. It's up the road. We're staying with him." Steve nodded his head while I continued the lie, "We went out for a walk. Didn't mean to walk so far." I looked at Steve, resisting the urge to wink.

Steve looked at the policeman. "Yeah, we better get back now. His dad gets worried when we're gone too long."

With that, the policeman offered us a ride to the house, which we gladly accepted. It would have looked suspicious had we refused. When we got to the house, I waved politely to the cop and yelled, "Thanks, officer!" in my best "good kid" voice.

Dad's house sat at the end of a long country road. I knew no one lived there. Dad had never rented it out or done anything with it after we left. At one time, the house had served as the warden's house for an old prison somewhere around the area. In my desire to escape, I'd never stopped to consider if the electricity was still on at the house. Of course, it wasn't. Or, if there was food of any kind. Again, there wasn't.

And, worse, by that time in the evening, the cold had settled in. The big, drafty house was colder inside than outside. Luckily, we thought, we had our lighters on us. We gathered everything we could to burn in the fireplace—old newspapers, a wooden chair, even some of Dad's old documents, not considering if they were important papers he might need to keep.

Nothing proved enough to keep the fire going through the night, and we spent the time until daybreak shivering and cursing our stupid idea to run away without planning ahead. At daybreak, we left, hoping to catch a ride back to Jacksonville. We were cold and tired and hungry.

Our great adventure had been a bust, but no amount of lack of sleep or food could make me swear I'd never do such a thing again, that I'd never attempt escape. Next time, I decided, I'd be smarter about it.

When we got home, Mom was frantic. I hadn't called her at any point along the way there or back, and she'd freaked out and called the worst possible person she could—my father. I hadn't wanted him to find out. I guess I thought no one would notice me gone. Magical thinking, again. I'd escape and no one would even give it a second thought.

Dad demanded to know where I'd been. I couldn't tell him burning papers and breaking chairs for kindling at his house in Georgia. So, I told a whopper of a lie about Steve and me spending the night at some friend's house that we sort of knew, though we couldn't remember his last name or what street he lived on. Dad yelled his head off for a while but, eventually, calmed down.

After the escape attempt, Steve was off limits.

For a short while, I went back to live with Dad but that didn't last long. Soon, I returned to Mom, Billy, Mark, and Joel. As summer ended, talk around the apartment turned to Starke, Florida. The new plan would be to move to Starke, where Mom had a male friend who could help her get set up in a house big enough for all of us, and I could start school in a new place, even a new county. That year had been tough on everyone. We'd all get a fresh start. A clean slate.

Yeah, that was the plan.

Life is a long lesson in humility.

J. M. BARRIE

CHAPTER 8

Starting Over

I F YOU'VE NEVER BEEN THERE, STARKE IS THE TYPICAL podunk, country town. Good, solid people but rinky-dink compared to living in a big city. For me, at fourteen and used to lots of city activity, moving to Starke was a bit of a culture shock, not that I considered Jacksonville the big time or anything.

Of course, I'd spent time in Hortense, Georgia, with Dad, Carolyn, and her kids, which was smaller than Starke, but in Hortense, I'd been too preoccupied with Dad and his moods to worry about what to do for fun. Being pulled away from the neighborhoods I knew and the guys I hung with in Jacksonville threw me for a loop—but only for a short while. I'd fix that old familiar feeling of being out of place, a fish out of water, by finding myself a new bunch of buddies. One, appropriately, nicknamed Fish.

Once eighth grade started—my second go around, as Lake Shore Middle had finally done what no school previously had and failed me—I gathered myself a new running crew—a small collection of boys who smoked cigarettes, skipped school, and knew how to cause mayhem. The new crew would make me feel right at home.

Among my friends were the aforementioned Fish, whose real name was Edmund; Kurt Thorton, who wasn't quite as wild as I and whose father would later become my mother's fifth husband; and Star Tooth, nicknamed by me for his gold tooth with its star-shaped cutout and whose real name I don't remember. Fish, Kurt, and Star Tooth were the principal players during my time living in Starke in the eighth grade, along with Cheryl Murray, whose name, strangely, I remember clearly.

Kurt Thorton and I became close when his father Marion used to pick him up at our house after school. Kurt didn't skip classes as much as Fish, Star Tooth, and I did. If I felt especially wild, I got Star Tooth to steal MD 20/20, a brand of cheap wine, with me from a convenience store. We hid out in the woods behind the school all day, getting drunk and making each other laugh. MD stands for the wine's producer, Mogen David, but we, along with everyone else, called it "Mad Dog." It was cheap and harsh and effective, an easy drunk.

Fish was well dressed and came from a respectable, middle-class family, the type of kid who wore pressed blue jeans. I found myself spending lots of time at Fish's house with its stocked pantry and ready supply of snacks. Not only did he have the type of home I imagined I wanted for myself, but Fish also had an ample supply of pot. When I wanted to get high, Fish had the hook up. More and more, getting high or drunk occupied my world, taking a place in it almost like a friend. My buddies: drugs and alcohol.

Moving to Starke hadn't squelched my desire to escape. If anything, my desire to break free of my life intensified. Everyone around me seemed ridiculous and pointless. People ran in place like hamsters on a wheel, never getting anywhere. I didn't know anyone who had big goals or dreams, who talked of inventing things or becoming famous or making a difference, at least not in any real way, as if such things could happen. Even when I wasn't fully conscious of it, I had the sinking feeling that there was nothing for me, not here in the life around me. Not that I could see.

I wanted to be someone else, somewhere else. If I could have made myself disappear into some other life, I would have. Pot and alcohol helped me forget my life for a short while. It became my escape. I'd try in other ways, though. Like the time I ran away with Cheryl Murray and two boys I barely knew and whose name I don't remember.

Cheryl was the type of girl I gravitated toward, rebellious and ready for fun. Slender, with long brown hair, Cheryl attracted me but not just because she was pretty—like me, she was lost. The first time I saw her at school, she stuck out as a troubled kid, someone I could identify with. My attraction to troubled girls—and later troubled women—would be a pattern I'd repeat into adulthood.

Sometime around the early fall of that year, Cheryl found herself in serious conflict with her mother, enough so that she came to me and said she planned to run away. Just as it had been with Steve and taking off to Hortense, I jumped on the chance to hit the road. How the other two boys ended up with us is unclear. With my outgoing nature, I probably invited them along. The more the merrier.

Having no actual plan or place to stay and it being late in the day, the four of us decided it would be best to run away the following day. For that night, we'd break into the Bradford County Institute of Food and Agricultural Sciences office on the Farmers' Market grounds off US 301. Finding a way inside the old brick agricultural center was easy enough. There was no security alarm or guard. Not much happened in Starke, certainly not on the Farmers' Market grounds.

We broke into one of the small rooms kept for guys working the rodeos and fairground workers when the state fair came to town. Luckily, there was no rodeo or fair at the time. The room had a pair of twin beds and enough space to spread out comfortably, not that we slept much. Mostly, we spent the night smoking pot and telling stories, talking about how fantastic it'd be on our own.

In the morning, we made our way back to Cheryl's house to grab her some clothes and money she claimed she'd hidden in her room. In our rash decision to leave town, neither of us had considered getting her clothes and money the day before, and the reality of it hadn't dawned on her until she had no clean clothes to wear the next morning. The other boys and I didn't care if we had a change of clothes or not. We'd be fine leaving with the rags on our backs.

Going back to Cheryl's house proved to be a mistake. When we picked up her clothes and the few dollars she had, which turned out not to be much, a neighbor must have seen the four of us go into Cheryl's house in the middle of a school day and with her mom at work. We made it only a short ways from the house, walking down the railroad tracks that ran through the town, when two cops showed up. The nosey neighbor had called the police, we figured.

The cops spooked us, and in our panic, the four of us took off running. From the way they chased us, I soon figured maybe their showing up had more to do with breaking into the agricultural center than skipping school with Cheryl Murray. Maybe there'd been a report of the break-in. Four kids skipping school near the same area of town as the agricultural center looked suspicious enough to warrant questioning, especially after we bolted off.

The policemen chased us down the railroad tracks a good quarter mile—running a ways, then stopping, then running, then stopping. We'd run, then stop and check if they were still following. They were.

Finally, one of them pulled out his gun and fired into the air, which halted us in our tracks. I threw up my hands and told Cheryl to do the same. It was the first time I had handcuffs slapped on me, and I remember feeling like a tough guy, of being proud of myself in some twisted way.

The police took us to juvenile detention and questioned us for a long time. We admitted to breaking into the agricultural center. I didn't see what the big deal was since we hadn't stolen anything or destroyed property. We'd just spent the night somewhere.

I didn't start to get nervous until one of the officers questioned me about Cheryl, if any of us boys had "taken advantage of her." I was sophisticated enough to know right away what they were implying and knew we would be in a world of trouble if they thought we violated Cheryl or something. I knew we hadn't. Nothing sexual at all had happened with Cheryl, but I guess three boys and a girl alone together all night didn't look good.

Eventually, the cops believed us boys, along with Cheryl's own testimony, that nothing sexually inappropriate had occurred. However, the police charged us with breaking and entering, though the juvenile court later dropped the charges. Why, I don't know. Once again, I'd gotten away with poor choices and bad behavior, further cementing in my mind that I was free to do whatever I wanted.

A short time later, Mom married Kurt's dad, Marion Thorton, and went to live with Marion in nearby Raiford, Florida. For a short period, all of us lived together in Raiford. Eventually, Mark, Billy, and Joel stayed with Mom and Marion. Mom and Marion decided I'd stay with Kurt at Kurt's Uncle Owen's farm, so that we both could finish out the school year in Starke. Billy and Mark had already quit school and Joel hadn't started. It would be easier, all around, if Kurt and I lived on the farm with Kurt's uncle and aunt.

I enjoyed the farm and got along well with Kurt's Uncle Owen and Aunt Ann. Uncle Owen, as I called him, was a good ole boy who sold greens and other vegetables from the side of road. Uncle Owen and Aunt Ann didn't holler or fight, and there was always plenty to eat. Uncle Owen wore big overalls that stretched over his round belly and had a turned up nose that reminded me of a pig. I found him likeable and kind and was upset when I had to leave.

Within a month or so of living on the farm, Mom announced that she and Marion had bought a house in Keystone Heights, Florida, big enough for all of us, so I left the farm. For whatever reason, Kurt remained with his aunt and uncle. Less than fifteen miles southeast of Starke, off State Road 100, Keystone Heights was close enough that I could continue going to school in Starke.

School had been going okay so far that year. I skipped on occasion, mostly with Star Tooth, but I'd managed to keep my grades up enough to be passing. What would happen next would jeopardize passing eighth grade and send my life into chaos again.

I'd watched Billy and Gary pull off dine-and-dash scams back in Jacksonville numerous times. I'd even pulled a few of my own. None of us had ever gotten into any serious trouble over it. I suppose for that reason, I didn't think twice about doing the same thing in Starke.

Star Tooth and I had skipped school that day. Marion drove me to school each morning. When I didn't feel like going to classes, I met up with Star Tooth before the first bell and hightailed it off campus before any teachers or the dean got the chance to spot us. Usually, Kurt stayed at school.

In many ways, I was more advanced in my misbehavior than Kurt, who'd had a dad around and the attention of folks like Uncle Owen and Aunt Ann. Also, I knew Kurt didn't care much for Star Tooth. For whatever reason, I remember Kurt wasn't with us that day. If he'd been, he might have convinced me not to do what I did. Of course, as stubborn as I was, I doubt I would have listened.

The day itself was nothing extraordinary. Star Tooth and I bummed around town. At noon, we decided to order fries and Cokes at a local restaurant, some small place off US 301, where pulling off a dine-and-dash was easy. During lunchtime, the staff was usually shorthanded and too busy to notice us. We ordered and ate our meal, then left without paying with no problem.

The trouble didn't come until a few days later. I'd skipped school again. This time, Star Tooth wasn't with me.

I'd overlooked the middle-aged guy leaning against the front panel of his dark-colored sedan when I entered the convenience store. I'd been in the store for ten minutes or so, buying a soda or something. When I exited the store, I noticed the guy. A folded newspaper lay over his right hand. I glanced at the guy but didn't give him much thought. When I came within a few feet of him, he pulled back the newspaper and brandished a gun at me.

"Police. Hold it right there," he said. "Hands in the air."

I stopped immediately and raised my hands, dropping the unopened soda can. I couldn't make sense of it, though. I'd paid for the soda.

The undercover cop pulled out a badge, identified himself, and motioned for me to move toward his vehicle.

"Place your hands on the hood slowly," he said, "where I can see them."

I did as the officer told me.

The cop kicked the back of my right knee with his boot. "Now, spread your legs."

Handcuffing me behind my back, he patted me down while I tried to find out what he thought I'd done. Had someone inside thought I'd been stealing from the store? I tried to recall if I'd stolen from this convenience store with Star Tooth or Fish. I couldn't be sure I hadn't.

"What'd I do, officer?" I asked.

The cop placed me into the back of his vehicle while he radioed in to dispatch. Knowing the law as I did, I stopped talking and waited until we reached the Starke Police Department, which wasn't but a few blocks away. I didn't want to risk goofing up and incriminating myself somehow.

My dumb luck, it turned out a waitress who'd been at the restaurant where Star Tooth and I had made off without paying our tab a few days earlier had driven past the convenience store and recognized me hanging out in the store parking lot. She'd managed to contact the police. The undercover officer nearby made it there in time to detain me. Charged with "defrauding an innkeeper," a charge I wasn't even aware existed until then, I knew I wouldn't get out of this predicament easily. I was baffled that the police were making such a big deal out of fries and a Coke. Once again, I couldn't make sense of how my actions had consequences and that I was responsible for them.

Worse than the criminal charge, Mom called my father, who insisted on coming to the hearing date.

The hearing took place in juvenile court a few months later. By then, I'd turned fifteen and school was about to enter the fourth quarter. Not that I cared a lot about school, but I wondered how the case would affect moving on to ninth grade. I knew I couldn't quit school until I was sixteen, and I didn't want to get stuck in the eighth grade for the third time.

When I entered the courtroom, Star Tooth sat at the front table and glared at me. Mom walked beside me, Dad behind the two of us, dressed like a lawyer and carrying a tan leather briefcase. I wasn't surprised that Star Tooth was angry. We hadn't talked since my arrest. The waitress had told the police I was with another boy. I'd given up my friend to the cops, figuring it wouldn't take much for them to find out on their own.

My court-appointed counsel spoke briefly with my parents. Though the court had dropped the breaking-and-entering charge the fall before, my juvenile record didn't look good. I'd no idea what the court might do to me. Would I be sent away to a boys' reform school? Maybe I'd be sentenced to time in juvenile detention. My only hope was managing to talk my way out of trouble.

Unfortunately, the judge didn't care to hear what I had to say. Fortunately, however, he would listen to my father.

Dad had brought in the briefcase to "look official."

"Timothy, we're gonna take care of this matter," he said.

I don't know how effective the briefcase would be. I did know it was empty, which I found funny back then and still do today. Dad was always well dressed and immaculate in his appearance. At my hearing, his demeanor took on an even more polished look. Dad asked to speak directly to the judge and pleaded my case for me—and my counsel.

Standing before the judge, Dad laid his empty briefcase on the oak table. "Your Honor, we know that our son Timothy has made some bad choices lately." Dad's deep voice sounded concerned for me. I suppose he was, but I could tell that much of what he said was for the court. "I know my son can do right, and I intend to see that he changes his ways from now on."

We hadn't talked about what would happen after the hearing. I was starting to get the feeling my father was leading up to something I wouldn't like. There was no way, though, I could stop him from whatever he wanted to say.

"I think my ex-wife, Timothy's mother, has had a hard time of it with Timothy and that it's time for me to step in and help."

There it was. Whether he planned to or not, Dad was swearing to the court that if they dropped the charges, he'd make sure I got "set straight."

I wanted to look at Mom, ask her what was going on, but I couldn't. Again, folks were making decisions without talking to me. Had my father and she decided I'd leave Starke and return to Jacksonville with him? I knew I couldn't stop it if I wanted, but the thought of leaving with him terrified me.

Life with Mom and Marion and Kurt and my brothers was okay. I didn't want to leave, not that I felt a strong attachment to them or the town; it wasn't like that. If I didn't stay with them, I knew it meant living with my father—returning to chaos and madness, never knowing when he'd explode in anger and violence.

Before I knew it, my father had convinced the judge that the best thing for me was to leave town and promise never to come back. I'd go back to Jacksonville with him and finish the school year in Duval County. The judge was more than happy to agree to the arrangement. My father had stepped in and saved me from a boys' home or juvenile detention.

Now, who would save me from my father?

Out of suffering have emerged the
strongest souls; the most massive characters
are seared with scars.
KAHLIL GIBRAN

CHAPTER 9
Life in Hell

ALMOST IMMEDIATELY, MY FATHER WHISKED ME BACK to Jacksonville.

We didn't stay for long. For his own reasons, which he didn't share, my father decided that he and I would live in Yulee, north of Jacksonville. I would finish out the school year on his watch, virtually on lockdown. He'd stay home on leave from the Merchant Marines and live off his savings. The problem of what to do about Timothy had been solved.

The next few months were a living hell.

My father's drug and alcohol abuse had continued while I'd lived in Starke, and, from what I could tell, had only gotten worse. The sickness that he suffered from and his irrational behavior made living with him like navigating a land mine field. One misstep and . . . explosion!

When he wasn't intoxicated, Dad could be fine. People found him interesting, charismatic, a real character. The prolonged drug and alcohol abuse warped his real self, twisting him into some dark version of himself. I would have loved to have known him as a sober man. I loved him, but his unpredictable reactions, emotional abuse, and desire to control those around him made life together intolerable.

When I wasn't at school, I was either at home or with Dad at his friends' houses in Oceanway, in Jacksonville's Northside. Dad would take me to Oceanway with him, where he'd drink and smoke pot with his friends until all hours of the night. I'd sit on the couch—sometimes watching TV but mostly just watching all of them—trying not to be seen or heard. Invisible. If Dad was interested in what his friends were doing, then he wasn't interested in me, which suited me fine.

While living in Yulee, I first witnessed my father smoke marijuana. I'd been doing it for years and knew he did, but he'd never smoked it around me. Once, driving home from one of his trips to Oceanway, he lit up a joint. Dad had an old black van at that time, one with a column-mounted gearshift. He was always buying old cars. Immediately, the distinct odor of cannabis filled the van. I pretended not to notice.

After a few minutes, my father handed the joint my way. "You want some?"

His question shocked me, and I wrestled with how to respond. "What's that?" I asked, pretending not to know.

"Don't mess with me, boy. You know what this is." Dad pulled the joint back and took a hit. He inhaled deeply, holding the hit a few, long beats, then exhaled. "I know you've been smoking it."

He held the joint out a second time. Tentatively, I took it from him. The feeling was odd, sitting beside my father, taking hits, sharing a drug experience.

In the back of my mind, I knew it was wrong, that we'd crossed a line. I tried not to think too much about it. For a long while, that was it, one shared joint. Eventually, we'd smoke pot together on occasion. More often, he'd ask me to score some for him. Another line crossed. The boundaries of what constituted proper parental behavior got murkier and murkier. My father had taken me away from my mother and Starke to set me on the right path. Now, this was the path he'd chosen.

SCHOOL BECAME A CHANCE FOR ME TO ESCAPE THE oppressive power of my father. I tried to do well to keep him happy. Dad demanded I come right home afterwards, which I did. If he hadn't been drinking, the evening might go okay. When he'd been drinking, though, I knew I could have a hard time of it.

The trips to Oceanway stopped after Dad came home late one night, his shirt covered in dark red smears I knew could only be blood. He had that look in his eyes, the one that told me to stay clear and quiet. He said something about someone having upset him at his friend's house. I wasn't sure if he'd beaten someone up, or stabbed someone, or worse. We never went back to Oceanway again.

As the time in Yulee progressed and the end of the school year grew closer, I hoped my father's mood would get better. It didn't. The slightest wrong word or inflection in my voice that sounded disrespectful to him would set him off. He'd launch into a rant about how much he was forced to put up with for me. He made it clear that he hated living in Yulee, that he was doing it only for me, that his life was miserable because of me. I'd put so much grief and worry and stress on everyone—Grandma, him, my mother—that he didn't know how he could bear it all.

Just as it had been with Grandma when I was little, I was the cause of all his problems. As when he'd yank me out of bed at midnight and take off down the road, running from his mother who was "killing him," now I was "killing him." He made it clear, day in and day out, that I was the problem. I was worthless and no good and ruining his life. Even though I tried not to let it happen, the words cut me, a thousand slices, each word a blade.

One particular evening stands out vividly in my mind. Dad had been drinking. I don't remember what exactly set him off. I recall that I was sitting at a table in the small kitchen of the furnished house he'd rented for us. Dad was cooking dinner, steak or pork chops or something like that. I sat at the table while he stood over the stove. He'd just picked up a large serving fork to turn over one of the steaks or chops, whatever was in the frying pan. For some reason, he thought I'd mouthed off to him. I guess that maybe I'd raised my voice or something, though I don't recall having done so.

In a flash, he dove across the kitchen table, tackling me to the ground. I was fifteen and a good size, but in an instant, he transformed me into a child again. Tears sprung to my eyes as he held the serving fork to my throat. A terror nearly indescribable swept though my body. Instantly, I began to beg him not to hurt me.

I tried not to look him in the eyes, knowing that would only anger him further. "I'm sorry, Daddy. I didn't mean it." Even though I didn't understand what I'd done wrong, I begged him to forgive me for it.

"You don't raise your voice to me after all I'm doing for you!"

I could feel the heat of my father's rage.

"You don't disrespect me in my home!"

"You're right, you're right," I whimpered.

Often, my only tactic was to agree with him, hoping he'd calm down and back off, much as he'd done with the black man on the bridge years before.

The move worked. He took the serving fork from against my throat and stood up. I straightened the upended chair and table and spent the rest of the night humbling myself, agreeing with him, and apologizing for being so much trouble. We never ate the dinner he'd cooked.

Like the man on the bridge, to whose head my father had held a gun, I needed only to give up and submit, and he would back off. During probably the most horrific moment living in Yulee, even that survival tactic I feared would not be enough.

WHAT I REMEMBER OF THE INCIDENT IS BEING ON THE on bridge—in the passenger seat of my father's black van—riding from Yulee into Jacksonville. I don't remember what took place before or after, or where we were going or why. Some moments are like that. Perhaps the chemicals that flood the body in times of extreme fear are so strong that we forget. The moment sears into our brains, but the particular details lie beyond our reach, our brain doing its best to protect us.

We were on a bridge. Not a long one, as with the Sister's Creek Bridge, but long enough. I remember looking at the water, knowing for sure that this time he'd do it. He'd kill us both, jerk the wheel and send us careening over the edge to our deaths. Whatever happened must have started before the bridge because by the time we got to it, he was already in full rage mode.

My father's hands gripped the steering wheel of the black van, his eyes bulging. "I'm gonna to do it, Timothy! I'm gonna kill us both!"

I begged him not to hurt us. I don't even know what I said, what I promised to do differently. I'm sure I told him how awful I was and how right he was, anything to stop him from yanking the driver's wheel. That day his rage was beyond any level I'd seen before.

He repeated his violent mantra, "I'm gonna do it! I'm gonna do it!"

His speed increased as we reached the top of the bridge. I shut my eyes and braced for the inevitable. I was going to die.

At some point coming down from the top of the bridge, I blacked out.

I NEVER SPOKE TO MY FATHER ABOUT THAT DAY ON the bridge or in the kitchen. He never brought it up, and neither did I. I suppose his feelings of isolation, frustration, and anger reached a boiling point in Yulee. His life had become so unmanageable that he lashed out at whatever was closest at the time. Unfortunately, it happened to be me.

We packed up and left Yulee the day school let out for the summer, returning to Grandma White in Jacksonville. Even if my father's drug and alcohol abuse continued, at least I'd be closer to my grandmother who I knew loved me and to the streets of Jacksonville with which I was familiar.

The return was a mixed blessing.

The sanity of society is a balance of
a thousand insanities.
RALPH WALDO EMERSON

CHAPTER 10
A Big Mix of Crazy

Sin City hadn't changed during my absence. The rough neighborhood of Jacksonville was a crazy mix of dysfunction on many levels, but also ripe with comfortable pleasures for me. I felt right at home hanging out with the types of guys I was familiar with, smoking pot and running the streets. Freed from the prison that was Yulee, I quickly fell into a familiar pattern, picking up three friends who constituted my core group of partying buddies.

Raymond, Robbie, Dewayne, and I started drinking Lord Calvert, popping quaaludes when we could get our hands on them, and tripping on hallucinogenic mushrooms from the Skinner Dairy fields near Sin City. Drugs became my chief means of making myself feel better about all the dysfunction around me, a way to calm the storm.

Moving to Yulee with Dad had put a greater strain on our relationship, but at least my restricted environment helped me pass the eighth grade. Having seen Billy and Mark both drop out after turning sixteen, I figured I'd do the same. Certainly, I hadn't gained any newfound sense of direction or ambition since having left my last school in Duval County. I had thought, however, that I'd at least make it to the official drop out date of my sixteenth birthday, but that wouldn't be so.

DAD STARTED SPENDING TIME WITH A WOMAN NAMED MYNA, whom everyone called Bird. Myna had a daughter about my age named Renee, a pretty girl who liked older boys.

Dad seemed calm around Myna and Renee, not as he had been with Carolyn, and I began to sense a pattern with my father. Dad was more content, easier to be around, when he was with people he chose to be in his life, rather than those who were there tied to some sense of duty or responsibility. My father had gotten Carolyn pregnant and so felt an obligation to marry her, as he had my mother. Both marriages had failed. With Myna and other women he wanted to spend time with, but wasn't obligated toward, he appeared much happier.

Unfortunately, I knew, and very much felt, that I was a duty, an obligation—not that he didn't in his own way attempt to meet that obligation but that it came at a cost to those around him, as well as to himself. No one had taught him or modeled for him how to cope with life. Drugs, alcohol, and anger became his coping devices, and his repeated abuse, I believe, led to deep psychological issues.

By this time, around ninth grade, I was developing my own psychological issues. Myna didn't smoke pot, but I remember sitting around Myna's kitchen table lighting up with my father. We'd had the one experience before, in Yulee, but since then we hadn't used together. It wasn't too long before he asked me to score for him. I think back now about how messed up and wrong that was for him to ask me and for me to oblige his requests. I'd concluded that his alcohol and drug use was a problem—though not one that anyone brought to his attention and demanded he change—but I had yet to see a connection between his substance abuse and my own.

Researchers believe that the brain halts development at whatever stage addiction begins. A person who begins abusing substances at a young age, by that reasoning, would remain at an adolescent level of development. I would discover later that my addiction stopped me from progressing beyond a juvenile way of thinking, with limited reasoning and ability to predict the consequences of my behavior. I believe now that my father's early drug and alcohol addiction in the Merchant Marines led to similar limited ability to reason and a way of looking at the world that fueled his resentment and left him ill equipped to solve daily problems in productive ways.

EVEN WITH MY REASONING DEVELOPMENT ON HOLD, I managed at this time to make some progress. I secured a job washing dishes at Sambo's Restaurant, a few blocks walking distance from Sin City, and fared well enough in school. The dishwashing job allowed me to sign up for the work program and put money in my pocket, a lot of which I spent on drugs. Smoking pot was an everyday thing by now, so it seemed no big deal to me to carry a bag of pot to school. Usually, I kept it rolled up in a baggie that I'd hide down my pants. On the day that led to my permanent expulsion from Duval County Public Schools, I'd stored it away in my front pocket instead.

I don't know if someone in gym class at Arlington Junior High saw me move the baggie of pot to my front pocket or how it all came to pass. At some point that class period, nonetheless, Principal Knight and Coach Podany stopped me on the basketball court, each grabbing me by an arm, and attempted to haul me off to the main building.

Principal Knight guided me by the arm off the court. "We have reason to believe you have drugs on your person."

"I don't know what you're talking about," I protested.

Of course, I knew exactly what they were talking about. It didn't look like, however, that I was going to be able to talk my way out of this one. Coach's grip on my arm was tighter than that of Principal Knight's, and I was able to pull away from him. In doing so, I inadvertently hit him. It wasn't intentional, but I landed a good whack. I hightailed it across the field, dumping the pot out and disposing of the baggie as I ran. When I finally made it home that evening, the police had come and gone. Principal Knight had contacted the authorities and reported the incident, including my striking him.

In the insanity of that period and the twisted relationship with my father, Dad concocted a story and encouraged my friend Andy Roberts to lie that I'd had pornographic pictures in my pocket, which accounted for my reluctance to be searched. Panicked, not meaning to strike the principal, I'd broken free and run. That was the story. The only part that was real was that I hadn't meant to hit anyone.

The county filed charges in juvenile court, expanding my arrest record to include illegal possession of drugs and assault. Principal Knight and Coach Podany testified, as did Andy. The resulting sentence was expulsion for life from Duval County Public Schools. The only bright spot in the whole mess came from my father, who appeared to be on my side, as misguided as his efforts to help my case were. I appreciated having Dad stand up for me, even if it included my friend committing perjury. The court didn't buy the story, anyway.

Shortly after the incident, my father rented a singlewide trailer in Sin City for me, not far from Grandma's apartment, in what I suppose was a measure to make me accountable for myself. Fifteen years old, expelled from school, and having no desire to return even had they reversed their decision, I packed up my few belongings and moved out on my own. This wasn't a point of discussion between Dad and me, however. Simply, one day Dad drove me to the trailer, showed me there were groceries in the fridge and cabinets, and wished me good luck.

Within a few weeks, I got work roofing for a local company, and Andy Roberts and his brother Johnny moved in. With me, the Roberts brothers, Raymond, Robbie, who was Raymond's older brother, and Dewayne, the trailer soon became party central. So much partying, in fact, you could cut the pot smoke with a knife. Drugs and alcohol were everywhere. Weed, of course, was abundant, but there were also mushrooms, acid, and pills. Cocaine wouldn't come around for a few more years, but whatever came along and felt good, we did. Everyone in Sin City about our age knew if a person was looking for a party, there was likely one happening at the trailer.

DAD AND GRANDMA WEREN'T BUT UP THE ROAD A WAYS, SO the idea that I was on my own didn't really sink in for a while.

Andy, Johnny, and I all worked and handed our money, minus our food, pot, and booze funds, over to Dad to keep the rent paid and electricity on.

Dad had rented the trailer after telling the landlord that the three boys he'd see there were his three sons and that he worked out of town a lot, but the boys would be home if he needed anything. Somehow, we kept the bills paid and had money left over for our entertainment, which was getting as high and wasted as possible.

Often, I'd come home from roofing to find a pot of stew or other meal from Grandma on the front steps of the trailer. I might be on my own, but Grandma still made sure I ate. Seeing those dinners warmed me with a sense of comfort and love. I knew that if I had Grandma around I could manage being on my own, even if I still had no real idea how to function. After all, I hadn't rented the trailer myself or gotten the electricity and water turned on. These things had been done for me. I was an adolescent thrown out into the world and trying to survive.

One thing that period did establish for me was gaining skills I'd later fall back on to help turn my life around and create a successful future. Across town, in more affluent neighborhoods, boys might go to college, become lawyers, doctors, and engineers. In Sin City, guys became roofers, construction workers, welders, and other tradesmen. It seemed inevitable that I'd start roofing. It was backbreaking work, but I liked it.

My first job as a roofer was as the kettle man, lugging five-gallon buckets of hot tar onto the flat roofs. The buckets were heavy, and I was glad when my supervisor gave me the chance to start shingling pitched roofs. Learning the trade came easily for me, and soon I was laying shingles with the best of them.

The only downsides to my experience living in the trailer were my growing reliance on drugs and alcohol and watching those around me who appeared to be turning into addicts already at such a young age. Getting away from Dad on a daily basis eased my general discomfort with life and the pressure I felt having to tiptoe around his aggression, but it also allowed for more freedom than I could responsibly handle. In his own way, Dad would come over to "check up on me," strolling into the trailer carrying his shotgun, placing it on the kitchen table, and asking me and the boys questions. Were we behaving ourselves? Were we getting up for work in the morning?

I remember one time when Dad came in with the shotgun he'd taken to toting around, along with the guns he usually carried.

He laid the gun on the kitchen table. "You boys minding yourselves?"

I looked to the boys, giving them the *be respectful* look.

"Yes, sir," I said.

"Good." Dad looked at each of us, then at the table. "You know I could kill you boys with any item on this table."

Not a one of us flinched or opened our mouths, but we all stared at the shotgun.

Silently, I thought, *Please don't kill my friends.*

Dad went on. "You see this pen? I could stab you in the brain with this pen . . . kill you in an instant. You ever see a man kill someone with a pen?" Dad looked at the shotgun. "Don't need a gun. Anything can be a weapon in the right hands."

Dad made it a point to show up from time to time and remind us that even though he wasn't around, he was still very much in control and top dog of the trailer. Sometimes, his voice even seemed to growl, putting us in our place were we to dare and be less than one hundred percent respectful. The guys knew without me having to say so that they'd be wise to watch themselves around my father.

After Dad married a lady named Dot when I was sixteen, whom he met about the time he rented the trailer for me, he calmed down considerably. He no longer carried the shotgun and talked about killing people with household objects. Dot's life before Dad had been what I would call *normal.* Her husband had passed away and, like Carolyn, she was raising her three children on her own. Unlike Carolyn, she was not pregnant by my father when they married, and she seemed to have a calming effect on Dad.

Dad moved in with Dot and her children after the wedding. From the start, I got along well with her kids, later living with her son Brad for a short period. Their marriage ended after a number of years together, but they remained friends long after.

A Big Mix of Crazy

THE PARTY AT THE TRAILER ENDED WHEN JOHNNY ROBERTS got his girlfriend Karen pregnant and took off for Texas, leaving his brother angry at his actions and us without a third person to help pay the bills. It didn't concern me too much though. I'd soon discover another trailer. The party would move from one location to another, just a minor bump in the road.

Grief is the price we pay for love.

QUEEN ELIZABETH II

CHAPTER 11

Love and Loss

The first time I laid eyes on Julie, I fell for her. I fell hard. Her long blonde hair and blue eyes left me tongue-tied.

Julie was my friend Greg Simmon's younger sister. She'd just quit school and hung out with Greg and me at our friend Richard Harding's trailer. Richard was a few years older than we were and had recently lost most of the fingers of his right hand in a work-related accident. He was at home recovering, self-medicating for his physical and emotional pain from the accident with drugs and alcohol.

The relationship between the Roberts brothers had gone bad when Johnny moved in his girlfriend and got her pregnant. Life at our trailer had grown difficult and Johnny's departure to Texas meant Andy and I needed to bring in another contributing roommate or find somewhere else to live. Greg and I decided it would be best to move in with Richard, to give him friends to help in his physical recovery and keep his mind off the accident. We figured the best way to do that was to keep a nonstop party going. I wasn't mature enough to know what my friend really needed.

Julie and I quickly became a couple, my first steady girlfriend. I didn't handle it well. Models for healthy romantic relationships had been rare. I'd witnessed Kurt Thorton's aunt and uncle, who got along well and spoke kindly to one another, and Granddaddy Carl seemed to have a good relationship with Grandma Taylor. For the most part, the relationships I saw were fraught with arguing, distrust, and inequity. For the first several months, our young love was wonderful, but it wasn't long before my insecurities and petty jealousy put a strain on the relationship.

I feel bad about it now. Julie was a good girl and very loving, but I was inept at working out problems or sharing my feelings productively. Often, I gave into my own fears, accusing her of flirting with my friends and trying to control her behavior. Even after she moved into the trailer with us, I couldn't shake the feeling that maybe she didn't really want to be with me, maybe I wasn't good enough for a girl like her. I found myself creating scenarios in my head about her with other guys. When friends would come over, I kicked her under the table, just hard enough to get her attention, if she looked at or talked to another guy in a way I thought was wrong. I wasn't physical with her, besides the attention-getting kicks, but I know that my behavior was inappropriate and a cover-up for my own immaturity and emotional problems.

After a few months together, Julie and I moved into my Uncle David's small apartment behind his home. Uncle David had built a detached unit, one bedroom and one bath, behind his home in Sin City, about a mile from Grandma White's apartment. He invited us to move into the unit. We were happy to be on our own, playing grown-ups, living together like a real married couple, though she was only sixteen and I was seventeen. To help even further, Uncle David loaned me four hundred dollars to buy my first car, a 1964 Galaxy 500. Moving into Uncle David's place, however, did little to curb my insecurity or poor decision making.

In particular, I remember my eighteenth birthday. Julie had been sweet to bake me a cake. The plan was that I'd come home from work and we'd eat dinner and spend the evening in together. I was still roofing and the guys had suggested we go out after work. I can't blame it on the guys I worked with, though. I knew Julie was waiting on me. I knew she'd baked me a cake and wanted the evening to be special. I suppose her feelings didn't matter to me as much as drinking and partying.

Around midnight, I opened the front door to the apartment, where Julie waited cake in hand. Before I could say anything, offer any excuse, she shoved the cake into my face. Chocolate icing stuck to my eyes and hair. She walked away silently as chunks of yellow cake fell to the carpet. My selfishness had ruined everything for her. We made up, but, to this day, I still feel bad that I put my wants over her feelings.

My addiction was beginning to affect my relationships negatively. I knew then that she deserved better, but that didn't make me stop drinking and using. I knew I wanted to be a different person, be a better person, but I had no idea how to go about it. Deep inside, I always had the feeling that there were things I didn't know that I should have. I was aware that things should be different than they were, but how to put that into action escaped me.

My life was reactionary, living day to day, moment to moment. Whatever popped into my head to do, I did. There was no thinking through decisions or looking beyond the action to consequences. None of that reasoning existed for me. I was living truly in the moment but not in a good way, and the only moral principle I possessed, the only thing that kept me somewhat straight, was the fear of getting caught. At some point, even that principle disappeared.

When I decided to rob the Sonny's Bar-B-Q, I was driving home from a friend's house high as a kite. Julie had bought me a buck knife for my nineteenth birthday just three days prior. I had it on me, as I pulled behind a bar adjacent to the restaurant.

Around one o'clock in the morning, the closed restaurant looked easy enough to break into. Not wanting to leave fingerprints, I looked around my car for something to cover my hands and came across a pair of socks. Around the back of the restaurant, I pulled the socks over my hands, then broke out a side window with my roofing hatchet and climbed through.

Inside, I rummaged around the front counter and office looking for whatever. Money, I guess, though I hadn't broken in with the idea of stealing money. The next day was payday, and I had enough money to buy the drugs I wanted. To this day, I've no clear reason for why I did it. I didn't want to get caught, at least not consciously. The decision was spontaneous and entirely ill conceived.

Within minutes, I heard noises outside. I ran to the front window and pulled back the curtain. In my foolish idea to rob the place, I hadn't even considered an alarm. A silent alarm had sent the cops my way. I scurried to find somewhere to hide and crawled into a waist-high commercial refrigerator, pulling the top down carefully as not to let it latch, possibly trapping me inside.

I heard the cops as they came into the restaurant and searched the premises. I tried to remain as still as possible. Maybe they'd pass by the cooler without noticing it was open.

As I prayed for them to leave, a cop opened the cooler and pointed his 12-gauge shotgun at my head. "Don't move! Don't move!"

Around the cooler, I could hear the other officers yelling similar commands. Eventually, the cop with the shotgun told me to move slowly out of the cooler.

In panic mode, I'd forgotten I'd opened the buck knife upon entering the restaurant and placed it in my back pocket. When I climbed out of the cooler and went to lay face down on the floor, the knife fell open, clanking onto the wood floor. Next came the *click, click, click* cocking of shotguns. For sure, I knew they were fixing to shoot me.

Thankfully, they didn't, instead arresting and booking me for burglary. Julie and my dad visited me in jail. This was my first time in adult jail. I remember talking to Julie through the small speaker on the other side of a plexiglass window. My heart broke seeing her on the other side of the glass, separated from me. I'd screwed up royally and failed her. Now we were without one another because of my dumb decision.

Bail was set a month later for twenty-six thousand, and my father arranged for a bail bondsman to secure my release. At first, I plead not guilty, but then petitioned the court to change my plea to guilty. The court sentenced me to four years probation, a five-hundred-dollar restitution fee, and ninety days in jail on work release. Between my initial release from jail and returning to court to plead guilty, I found employment suitable to the court with Arlington Builder Center. The man who hired me, Mitch T., would become a pivotal person in my journey through addiction to recovery.

DEALING WITH MY CONVICTION WASN'T THE ONLY ROUGH spot during this time. While on work release, an event would occur that would change the lives of several people around me and affect me in ways I would not come to understand fully for years.

Since coming home from Yulee with my father and moving into the trailer in Sin City, Raymond Wilkes had been my best friend. More than a friend, he'd been like a brother to me. Raymond was a big guy that scared everyone, except me. I loved Raymond and his tough-guy attitude. He'd find the biggest, ugliest, meanest dude in any crowd or situation, walk right over, and start a fight, always whipping the guy's tail, just to prove he was the baddest guy there. Raymond's oldest brother, Robbie, was almost as hotheaded, but not even he could start a fight the way Raymond could.

The Wilkes brothers fought like nothing I'd ever seen, so surprising, too, because I know for a fact they loved each other fiercely. Yet, when the two of them got together, especially when they were drinking, the best bet was that someone would end up bloodied and injured. Already, they'd had several major knockdown-dragouts. On one occasion, Robbie knocked Raymond's front teeth out. On another, he knocked Raymond in the head with a large beer stein, causing him to require over 100 stitches. Robbie was only defending himself. Raymond could fight better than Robbie and would beat the tar out of his brother when the mood overtook him, sometimes stripping the hide right off of him, even leaving lifelong scars on Robbie's forehead.

While I waited for my court date on the burglary charge, I stayed off and on with Robbie. Julie still lived with Uncle David but seemed to want less and less to do with me. Robbie was a few years older than I, was a carpenter, and had a trailer with an extra bedroom. It was in my bedroom at Robbie's trailer, while I was on work release, that Robbie shot his brother Raymond's left leg off.

Both drinking, the brothers got into one of their violent fights. The argument escalated and Robbie, to defend himself from his brother, took his 12-gauge double-barreled shotgun and shot Raymond in the leg. Remarkably, no criminal charges were filed. I suppose that their reputation with the authorities and history of violence toward one another left the police to rule it a case of self-defense.

MY CRIMINAL BEHAVIOR PUT A STRAIN ON MY RELATIONSHIP with Uncle David, who was disappointed in me for my actions and for hurting Julie. For a while, he hardly spoke to me. Julie still lived at his house, but it seemed he wanted nothing to do with me, and I bounced between living with Julie and living with Raymond, still recovering from the loss of his leg. What would soon happen would make the fact that I'd disappointed Uncle David even more painful.

I worked as a driver for Arlington Builder and Mitch. During work, I'd sneak off to see Julie, even though it was against the conditions of my sentencing. I missed her terribly and worried that she might find someone else. It killed me to discover when I returned home after the ninety-day stint that she'd slept with other guys. Of course, I'd cheated on her with her friends before breaking into Sonny's, but I couldn't stand the thought of her infidelity.

Not only had she been unfaithful, but she'd also hooked up with some folks at a bar that were into a new drug on the scene: cocaine. Neither of us had done cocaine before my going to jail. She assured me it was a fantastic high. With her, I snorted coke the first night out from work release. She was right. It was fantastic. I'd never felt a stronger, more amazing rush. Cocaine made me feel invincible. The mistake of the robbery and failing Julie was over. Now, everything would be all right. Julie and I would be closer than ever and all our indiscretions would be behind us.

Things were okay for a short while, a few months, then came New Year's Day and Uncle David's murder.

ON JANUARY 1, 1982, UNCLE DAVID LEFT A BAR WITH A MAN he'd met that day. In Uncle David's home in Sin City, the man struck him repeatedly on the head with a hammer. Grandma White, who sensed something wrong with her boy, found Uncle David dead in his home around 4:00 A.M.

Bank cameras showed the man with my uncle earlier the day before, New Year's Eve, withdrawing money from Uncle David's account. A bartender and server at the bar witnessed the two that evening, leaving together in the early hours of the morning. Just before dawn, Grandma "got her feeling," as she reported to the police, and walked the mile from her apartment to Uncle David's house, on the other side of Sin City. Inside, she made the gruesome discovery.

The news devastated us, especially Grandma who was beyond distraught. Authorities apprehended the man, Dennis Derrell Morrisett, eventually sentencing him to life in prison. Uncle David's death left Grandma a wreck. When I'd visit, I'd find Grandma at her kitchen table crying. This went on for over a year. Overnight, she became an old woman, inconsolable in her grief.

My uncle's death had an odd effect on my father. Dad would often warn that Grandma would not survive his brother's death; the tragedy would claim her as well. In his tone, I heard something darker, something accusatory toward me, as if I had any part in what had taken place. Perhaps he believed that if Julie and I hadn't lived in Uncle David's apartment, the murder wouldn't have happened. I couldn't understand why he wanted to make me feel guilty of the crime. Was it his way of continuing to control me?

Dad was the one to clean up his brother's house after the murder. Afterwards, he moved in. How he stayed in the house, I can't understand. I certainly didn't want to be inside it again; neither did Grandma.

In a bizarre twist, just after the murder, before police discovered the killer, officers questioned me about Uncle David's death. Where had I been that night? Did I know that folks were saying my uncle had tried to pay some neighborhood guys to beat me up? I'd heard the rumors myself afterwards, though I had no idea if they were true. I knew Uncle David had hard feelings about my behaviors that affected Julie. He'd always liked Julie a lot. I'd had no clue whatsoever that he'd wanted me hurt. I couldn't fathom such a thing.

With Uncle David's murder, Grandma's pain and grief, and my father's odd behavior and continued substance abuse, I pressed even harder to connect with Julie. I'd be a good boyfriend to her, I vowed. I'd work hard and take care of both of us. I'd stay straight and make some future for us.

At least in all my misery, I had Julie . . . and I had cocaine.

But pain insists upon being attended to.
God whispers to us in our pleasures, speaks
in our conscience, but shouts in our pains:
it is His megaphone to rouse a deaf world.
C.S. LEWIS

CHAPTER 12
Cocaine

CONTRARY TO THE ERIC CLAPTON SONG BY THE SAME title, cocaine *does* "lie."

The lie of cocaine is that it puts you on top, pushes you to new heights, lets you "ride on." All lies. I became addicted to the lies.

I loved cocaine, what it did, how it made me feel. On it, I soared to new heights. The problem with soaring is that what goes up must come down, and the fall isn't just a physical one—it's an emotional one, a spiritual one. Addiction lies to us and tells us we're okay doing what we're doing. We're special and deserve to engage in our addiction. We're beyond the scope of normal human behavior and consequences. We may see dysfunction in others, but our addiction lies to us and covers our dysfunction and disease from our eyes, even when it's as plain as day, even when it's right up in our face.

I loved Julie. I loved my grandmother. I still loved all my family, including my father. Yet, there came a time in my addiction when I loved drugs and alcohol more. Substances didn't judge me, didn't expect from me. Using was about having a good time.

To me, I saw no negative in cocaine. I bought into the lies—hook, line, and sinker.

JULIE HADN'T DONE COKE UNTIL MY INCARCERATION FOR THE Sonny's Bar-B-Q break-in. While I served time, she hooked up with a guy named Hank, her best friend's brother. She'd known Hank for years but only now gotten close. Julie had never been a big partier. Running with Hank introduced her to a new world of heavy drugs and the bar scene.

To us, dust was a rich man's drug, so even after I tried it with Julie, we didn't have the money to do it often. We could buy quaaludes for five bucks a pop or smoke pot all day for less money than a line of coke. It wasn't until I left my job at Arlington Builder Center to work beside Mitch, who'd left to work for another building materials business, that my cocaine use took off—thanks in part to the company owner's son. I hadn't worked for my new employer very long when the guy caught my attention.

Only the two of us in the shop, the owner's son walked up to me. "Hey, I want to show you something."

I had no idea what was up but followed him to the back office, where he opened a briefcase containing an ounce of cocaine. I'd never even seen an ounce of coke.

"Here, try this out." He handed me a small vial of the powder.

I took it, snorting it right there. With easy access to the drug, I was soon snorting coke everywhere: home, work, clubs, where it was nothing to party all night.

Sixteen years my senior, Mitch became my mentor of sorts, providing advice and support, but even Mitch couldn't stop me from diving nose first into cocaine and the lifestyle it presented. Mitch was different from anyone I'd spent much time around. Educated, well dressed, and financially secure, he offered a glimpse into the kind of life I found attractive. He was willing to put in the effort to get to know me and instill in me values I should have gotten as a child but didn't.

On the other side, though, was the owner's son—his flashy lifestyle and the fantastic high of cocaine. I suppose I wanted that lifestyle almost as much as I wanted the drug itself. At the club, I shone. Clearly the most interesting person in the room—or, when high, so I thought—I was the coolest dude, the funniest entertainer, the handsomest stud. Dang John Travolta on the dance floor, though I probably looked like a fool. It didn't matter because I was living the lie, and all around me were others caught in their own lies and dysfunction.

By that point, I'd been out of jail a year. Julie and I were growing further and further apart. She'd been with other men while I'd sat in jail and that gnawed at me, not that it should have with all the running around I'd done on her before my incarceration. At the clubs, I made up for it, in spades. There was no shortage of women offering sex to a guy with coke. Eventually, Julie met a guy in Daytona's Bike Week and took off to Chicago with him.

After she left, my cocaine use escalated. I wanted more and wanted it more often, but my salary amounted to a few hundred dollars a week. The expense of my addiction was catching up with me.

Luckily—or unluckily, I suppose—I hooked up with a girl named Tammy, a gorgeous girl but a full-blown cokehead, who introduced me to her dealer, James, a well-connected player with big, black tree limbs for arms and a thick neck. James must have seen the natural salesman in me.

He walked up to me in the club. "Hey, you want to do some business?"

That night he fronted me an 8-ball with the intent that I'd sell it and pay him back. I turned the product without problem and soon sold for James on a regular basis.

Worries about how to afford my addiction ended—my goal wasn't so much making money as it was securing an endless and free supply—and I quickly became the go-to guy for cocaine around Playground South and the other nightclubs in Jacksonville. To my understanding, I was something I'd never been before: *important*. They called me The Snow Man, the man with the white magic powder everyone craved.

I was in the limelight and needed. More important, I was *wanted*.

Quickly, my entrepreneurial spirit kicked in, and I started making more money than I'd ever seen. Doing and selling cocaine became my whole life, my full-time job, and I crossed another invisible line.

While I was on the clock at work, I'd sleep in the back room, desperately trying to hide my activities from Mitch. I'd started there as a driver but worked my way up to inside sales. Though a great salesman, I hated being inside. The minutes at work dragged like some old, broken thing.

Fresh from vacation leave, I remember standing at the counter staring at the clock, the minutes tick, tick, ticking past, each tick feeling like a nail driven into a coffin, a death sentence. My first day back, I'd been on shift for maybe ten minutes.

I watched the second hand of the shop clock on the back wall, feeling each excruciating second. All I wanted was to get high. The sales floor was dead, and I hadn't any powder on me.

After another long ten minutes, I thought, *I'm done.* Without notice or word to anyone, even Mitch, I walked out the front door, jumped in my car, and left. I knew I was wrong, a worthless piece of crap, but staying there a second longer felt impossible.

My addiction became an obsession. I'd always wanted drugs and alcohol, but I'd never experienced before that level of need. All I could think of was using, from where and when my next fix would come. Julie had left me. I'd walked out on Mitch and my job. My relationship with my father had deteriorated to the point of nonexistence, and I'd no clue how to help my suffering grandma, still grieving the loss of her son. Cocaine grabbed hold of me and sunk its teeth into my soul. In my own way, however, I was still trying to manage my unmanageable existence.

THE FIRST TIME I SHOT COCAINE WITH A NEEDLE, I THOUGHT my head might explode.

I thought I'd never shoot up. I'd seen people stick needles in their arms and told myself I'd never be that kind of drug user. Snorting had been okay, reasonable, but the idea of needles seemed dangerous and pathetic. Shooting was a line I didn't want to cross.

Eventually, my frequent nosebleeds made the needle seem attractive, and after a while, the high from cocaine started to ebb. I needed more to get the same high, and shooting the drug, I figured, seemed a stronger, faster fix. I wasn't wrong—on all accounts: it was a more intense high, but it was also dangerous and pathetic.

By this time, the guys I'd hung around had started to pull away. My best friend, Raymond, was attempting to live a more normal life away from Sin City with his wife, who was straight-laced and had no interest in partying. I'd lived with them awhile, making concerted efforts to hide my heavy drug use, or, at least, I believed I could. It wasn't long before there was no hiding what I was doing. They asked me to move out after my late nights of dragging home cokeheads meant trouble keeping their lives in order. I spent the next several years bumping around place to place, crashing on friend's couches, shacking up wherever I could, pretty much making a nuisance of myself—though I hadn't the good sense and clear-headedness to understand that at the time.

It wasn't like Raymond and Robbie and the others didn't drink or use drugs. They all drank heavily and smoked pot, like we all had back living in the trailers of Sin City. Cocaine, though, changed things. In fact, I turned Raymond and the rest of the guys onto cocaine. Before me, none of them had ever done it. Though the guys snorted coke on occasion, that wasn't enough for me. It seemed I needed a fix more and more often. Eventually, I needed a more intense feeling, a feeling strong enough to push away the garbage in my life, all the disappointments and all my failings.

My desire for pleasure and escape brought me around a new crowd at the clubs, a group not content with the occasional hit or the weekend high, folks who preferred the needle to the nose. For all my talk about how I'd never shoot up, my addiction landed me in a place I didn't need to be but, no doubt, was my eventuality: an apartment with two beautiful girls and a hot needle.

The saying goes, "Hang around a barbershop long enough and you'll get a haircut." That's pretty much how it went.

The place was a crummy, little apartment in Arlington. I don't remember the girls' names, random girls I'd never see again. I'd met them earlier that night at Playground South, and they'd invited me back to their place. Really, it was simple. I liked the girls, and the distaste for the needle melted away with the promise of a great, new high and two pretty girls to share it with. In fact, at the early stage I felt some apprehension about mainlining cocaine. I didn't like needles and didn't know how to find and hit a vein. Having two attractive girls there made it seems less intimidating, less of a threat.

The girls were sweet about my jitters, not making a big scene, though I'm sure that I tried to act smooth about the whole thing. One took my left hand, guiding me to pump my fist to get the blood flowing. I watched in amazement as the other girl drew the cocaine she'd mixed with water into the needle, held the needle point up, and then flicked its side while she pressed the plunger to expel the bubbles that pooled at the top of the dose. The process seemed like a ritual—a wild and dangerous, but captivating, ritual.

The veins in my arms were hard to see, and I worried the girl with the needle might miss. She didn't. As the drug shot through my system— even as I watched her jack back the needle that caused a flash of my red blood to retract inside the tip—I let go my fears, letting the drug take me where it wanted to go and take me over.

There was no comparison between snorting and shooting cocaine. The immediate sense of elation and ease was like nothing I'd felt before, fantastic and unnatural. We partied all night, shooting up and drinking, being reckless and free from our inhibitions.

At first, I told myself I'd never do it again, still fighting with my disgust for needles. I was only twenty-two, too young—I assured myself—to get hooked on the needle. Yet, when I snorted a line, I wished it would give me the high I'd experienced with the girls in that rundown apartment. It wasn't but a few weeks before I found myself back around folks mainlining. I let them inject the drug into my willing veins. It would be a short period doing both, snorting and shooting, before I'd teach myself how to inject the needle, getting past the sting and burn, learning to find a vein.

The first time I tried on my own, only a few months later, was clumsy and painful and left me in an ugly frenzy, with burning knots where I'd missed a vein, blood dripping down my arm. I wanted the drug in my system so badly, needed it to take me on its crazy ride. I wanted what I'd felt with the girls, the elation and escape from my reality. The sight was absurd. I was a mess, popping knots and begging my friend Harold, who'd no better idea than I did how to find a vein, to help me jack up.

I'd gone to a place with shooting cocaine that no other substance had taken me. That first night with the girls opened a door for me that I crossed through willingly and, in doing so, handed my soul to the devil, the demon that was my addiction. There was no return after that night.

I had shot a demon into my arm—and it refused to leave.

Even when I wasn't high, the demon was with me now. With alcohol, pot, and other drugs—even with powder cocaine to a certain extent—I'd been able to keep a full-blown addiction at bay. The demon was there and I was feeding it, but I hadn't given it the source that would allow it to waltz in and strip me of all my defenses and good sense. That time was over. This dance was different.

It wasn't long before guilt and shame—at a level deeper than I'd ever felt before—came shuffling through the door. I shut out everything else, alone to lose my soul and self in my addiction.

Over the next year and a half, I still went to clubs, but my partying life transformed into something darker, riskier. To some degree, the type of people I hung around also devolved. I started shooting up in clubs and gas station restrooms, not caring where I used or with whom. I did anything to get high, including using my own product instead of selling it, which meant I couldn't pay back the dealers, resulting in several beatings at the hands of dealers or their thugs and, at least once, getting shot at.

My addiction had me on a leash, leading me where it wanted to go.

I could sense somewhere inside that this thing wasn't me, that the demon that was my addiction had taken control and was trying to kill me, but I was powerless to stop it. I had subjugated myself to the power of darkness.

Still, that little kid in me who'd gotten down on his knees in my grandma's backyard in Sin City and prayed for God's help hoped I'd get myself under control. For a while, I held onto hope that each time I went on a bender, staying drunk and high for days, I'd clean up my act and walk straight. I'd give up the cocaine and then I could drink whenever I wanted, like regular people did. The voice of me at six years old told me everything would be okay. I'd no idea on God's earth how to make it okay—how to go about the day-to-day business of being normal—but as long as I clung to that feeling of hope, I believed there might be a way up from the depth to which I'd sunk.

When Raymond Wilkes died on September 27, 1985—at twenty-four years old, victim of a boating accident—I told that little kid good-bye. He and I wouldn't meet again for another nine years.

Many of us spend our whole lives running
from feeling with the mistaken belief that
you cannot bear the pain. But you have already
borne the pain. What you have not done is
feel all you are beyond the pain.
SAINT BARTHOLOMEW

CHAPTER 13
Boulevard of Broken Things

THE SOUND OF PASSING CARS WHOOSHED IN MY EARS. Seconds later, an approaching vehicle blared its horn at me. In the dark, even with the aid of streetlamps that shined their light across the boulevard, I couldn't see the driver of the vehicle, a boxy four-door sedan. Rage flared inside me at the sound of the horn blasts: two short, followed by one long. The sedan set off a chorus of horns from other cars on both sides of San Jose Boulevard, an ugly, angry symphony. I stuck up a middle finger at them and screamed something vile and unintelligible.

I'd spent the last four days on a binge, not sleeping but maybe an hour or two. It was Sunday evening, and I was still wearing the same jeans and T-shirt I'd put on Thursday morning for work. For whatever reason, the boss on my current roofing job had paid us on Thursday instead of the typical Friday, which just meant I had a pocket full of cash and an extra day to rip and roar.

In my drug and alcohol-induced derangement, I'd no idea of the danger I'd put myself in, insisting my on-again, off-again girlfriend at the time, Carol, let me out on the street. Carol was happy to oblige. I'd gone from happy-go-lucky party guy to crazed dopehead. Having drunk all the liquor and ingested all the cocaine I could buy, first with my paycheck—

until that ran out—then by whatever means I could manipulate, begging and scamming from friends and coworkers, I eventually lost my senses in Carol's car, yelling and crying and scaring the hell out of her.

I'd have dumped me out on the street, too.

I wasn't there long before a police car pulled alongside me, about the same time a guy came running across the northbound lane. Traffic had come to a dead stop. Bright headlights kept me from making out the cars or their occupants, but I could feel their eyes staring at me, judging me.

Two policemen exited their vehicle, hands positioned on their guns, ready for whatever I might pull.

"That's him, officers," the guy from across the street yelled. Apparently, the guy had called 9-1-1, then ran across the street to point me out, as if the cops might have difficulty locating me. "That's the guy who's been cursing at cars in the middle of the road!"

The obviousness of the man's remarks struck me as funny, and I laughed wildly as I took a seat on the hard asphalt.

I turned to the man, mustered all my sarcasm, and spat out, "I sure want to thank you for your support, sir!" The man's protests regarding my behavior continued until, finally, I shouted into the night air. "Yeah, man, that's me! Lock me up! You got me!"

As one cop walked around my left side, the other commanded the man to stand back, then looked me squarely in the face and said, "What the hell do you think you're doing?"

I laughed like the madman I'd become and yelled, "I'm sunbathing!"

Sensing the cop to my left moving toward me, I laughed again and held my arms out, turning my face to the night sky, as if the sun would come out in sympathy to my lunacy and bathe me in its splendor.

I'd lost all grips on reality. When the police officer placed me into the back of his cruiser, I was thankful that at least in jail the law would stop me from my own insane obsessions and compulsions. Stop the madness for a moment. I could regroup. Get it together. Raymond had been dead almost a year, and I'd had a time of it, trying to get my mind wrapped around the fact that he was truly gone forever.

When I figured out the cruiser was heading toward the beach and not downtown, to the jailhouse, I got concerned.

The back of the cruiser smelled of stale sweat and undertones of booze and cigarettes. I registered that the smell was most likely me and stared out the window, trying to focus in my hazy drunkenness on familiar landmarks as we drove east on Beach Boulevard. My irascibility had cooled, leaving me suddenly sleepy, and I fought to keep my head up. Silent tears rolled down my cheeks, tasting of salt and desperation.

My slurred speech oozed thickly from my mouth. "Ofazir, where we goin'?"

"We're going to get you some help," he said.

In the cop's voice, I thought I heard a sound not too often encountered in the last several years, a sound I'd heard in the voice of Grandma White and my mother and Julie, but not for a long time: the sound of compassion.

Help. The word seemed foreign to me. A strange four-letter word in a tongue I couldn't speak or understand. Surely, I'd heard wrong. Help? What was that?

I'd heard a little about detox and treatment, scattered whisperings, but knew next to nothing about either. As weird as it sounds, I felt some immediate comfort. Just the thought that there might be help out there for me—someone who was so far gone—settled me for the moment. Maybe I didn't have to go through this anymore; maybe I could live again. A sense of security washed over me as I sat back in the cruiser and let them take me wherever they would.

THE NEXT SIXTEEN OR SO HOURS WAS A BLUR. I awoke to sounds of feet shuffling, unfamiliar voices, and a painful throbbing in my head. A familiar smell, antiseptic and stark, hit me, turning my already queasy stomach. I registered the smell: bleach. I didn't know where I was and had only a hazy memory of how I'd gotten there. The cop's words filtered through my blurry thoughts, *We're going to get you some help.*

As I sat up in the bed, really just a cot with a thin foam mattress, I tried focusing my eyes but couldn't. I placed my aching head in my hands to gather myself. After a minute or two, my eyes adjusted to the bright lights around me and I perceived the figure standing over me. I blinked and rubbed at my face, four days of beard grown in. My mind tried to make sense of everything around me as I stared at the figure's chestnut-brown cowboy boots.

A scratchy voice with a thick southern accent spoke. "You weren't doing too good last night, was ya?"

I continued to stare at the boots—elbows propped on my thighs, hands on either side of my stubbly cheeks—not ready to look up. "No, I wasn't."

Cowboy Boots sat down on the cot next to me. "You don't know where you're at, do ya?"

"No," I said, looking up to face him. "Where am I?"

The man stared at me, wide-eyed, with a silly grin plastered on his tan, wrinkled face. I got a good look at him: a small fellow with thinning, dirty blonde hair and bad teeth, dressed in street clothes.

"Man, you're in the cuckoo's nest!"

His words hit me like a ton of bricks. I sprung from the bed, taking a better look around. Lined against the wall opposite me were three cots like mine, and on either side of me, two additional cots: six in total. The room was nearly bare, except for the cots, two small tables and chairs that looked as if they might be bolted to the floor, and a metal cabinet with a large padlock keeping its contents secure.

A man sat on one of the cots on the other side of the room, talking to himself. Another man walked slowly in a circle in the center of the room, dragging his feet in an unnatural way, which accounted for the shuffling noise to which I'd awoken. Without further hesitation, I bolted from the room.

Outside, in a larger room, much like the lobby of a hotel—only *this place* was no hotel I'd ever stayed—several men in puke-green hospital gowns sat in chairs around a TV, an old wood console model. A few more walked aimlessly, in the same awkward shuffle.

I stood a moment in the center of the room, struggling to get my bearings. To my right was the area I'd just left, a long hallway measured by a series of evenly spaced doors on both sides, ending at a blank wall. More communal rooms with cots and bolted-down chairs, I figured. On the opposite end of the lobby, double doors awaited me. I headed straight for them, determined to leave.

I hit the metal door lever full on but, as much as I pushed down, the door wouldn't open. I was locked in.

I scanned the room again, near frantic. No one had said anything about *the cuckoo's nest*. I hadn't signed up for the crazy house, and no one was going to lock me away. I knew I'd partied too hard, but there was no way I was mentally insane.

At a desk in the center of the room, two facility staff talked between themselves. They seemed undisturbed by my struggle with the locked doors and paid me hardly any notice as I raced toward them.

"Man, I got to get out of here," I said to one of the staff, then turned to the other and said, "You got to let me out!"

I knew they could hear the desperation in my voice. The muscles in my gut seized, my heart threatening to pound from my chest. I'd only one thought: *to get on the other side of those double doors.* I'd made a terrible mistake letting the cops take me here, one that needed correcting right away. No one could know the police had shipped me to the loony bin, as I viewed it back then. I'd get out of here, then figure out how to correct whatever damage I'd cause during my binge.

The staff member I'd addressed first, a guy that looked to be in his midthirties, dressed head to toe in white, laid down a manila folder, then held his hand out like a stop sign. "Settle down. You're going to be all right."

"You don't understand . . . I don't . . . belong here," I said, struggling to catch my breath.

"It's going to be all right," he repeated.

The other staff member, a female nurse with a small waist and long black hair pulled back in a tight ponytail, chimed in. "You're under seventy-two-hour hold for attempted suicide." Her face wore a forced smile. "You're not going anywhere."

I stared at the two of them, one to the other, dumbfounded. The words *attempted suicide* echoed in my head. Finally, I gave in and stepped back, defeated. I'd done it now, gotten myself carted away. I took a seat in a chair furthest from the TV. Cowboy Boots was nowhere in sight.

I spent the rest of that morning and long into that first afternoon in the Mental Health Resource Center trying to figure out my next move.

OF COURSE I HADN'T TRIED TO KILL MYSELF, I EXPLAINED TO the Indian doctor, the staff psychiatrist, later that afternoon. By then, I'd settled down considerably, but my stomach and head still ached horribly and I'd developed a bad case of the sweats, withdrawal effects from my alcohol and cocaine use. I was too sick to want a drink yet, though I'd gotten to the point in my alcohol addiction where I drank every day, sometimes all day. This time, I told myself, I'd just gone overboard. I wouldn't do it again.

The psychiatrist's heavy accent made him difficult to understand. "And you are how many years old?" he said. He looked down at a chart, rapidly scratching notes as he ticked off questions in rapid fire.

"Twenty-four," I answered. "I was born February 3, 1962, same day as my dad." I didn't want to talk to the doctor, but maybe if I gave this guy information, showed him how rational I was, he'd let me go early.

"I see." The doctor scribbled more notes, head down in the chart. "What medications you are taking?"

"No prescriptions . . . ones from a doctor," I said.

"I see," the doctor repeated. "And how many glasses of alcohol you are drinking in a week?"

His question stopped me short. I knew he'd ask about drinking, but trying to figure how much I drank was impossible. I drank as much as I could.

"A lot," I said. "I don't know. A whole lot."

"And what else?" he said without missing a beat, face still in the chart. "Are you smoking? Are you abusing drugs?"

There was no escaping the ugly track marks on my arms. I sat along the desk in his office, in a hard metal chair, and copped to everything. Admitted to injecting cocaine, smoking pot, a whole list of any drug I could remember taking over the last six months. Maybe if I told this doctor it all, confessed to everything, I'd get rewarded time off for good behavior.

But, I wasn't in jail. The psychiatrist reminded me that I was in lock up for seventy-two hours and that the facility would not release me until that time was up, he pronounced me medically stable, and I was no longer deemed a danger to society or myself. I'd been involuntarily committed according to the Florida Mental Health Act, otherwise known as the

Baker Act, which allowed their facility to hold me. Then, he told me I had a drug and alcohol problem and explained about group therapy.

THAT EVENING AND THE NEXT TWO DAYS WERE A JUMBLE OF sad and pathetic images.

At dinner that evening, a man who was dying of AIDS sat next to me. A dozen or so of us "patients" sat around a long cafeteria table. The man, a skeletal figure with purple lesions on his arms and face, looked too weak even to carry the cafeteria tray.

I scooted over to make a place for him at the end of the bench seats. The look of distress on his face made me wish I could do something more for him. His hands shook as he tried to eat the meal, his hospital gown practically a tent on his emaciated frame. Halfway through dinner, I noticed he'd started to weep. I soon realized from the reaction of the staff on duty that the man had lost his faculties and urinated on himself.

THE SECOND NIGHT IN THE FACILITY WAS HARDER THAN THE first. That first night I'd been so exhausted and out of it, I'd passed out on the cot unaware of my surroundings. The second night, I knew exactly where I was and who my roommates were.

Though I still felt a bit queasy, my nerves had settled enough to fall asleep. I think I was the first in the room to crash. Sometime shortly after I nodded off, one of the men, an excitable, manic-looking fellow who liked to clap his hands repeatedly, climbed onto my bed.

Startled awake by the man standing on the foot of my bed clapping his hands wildly, like an excited monkey, I freaked out. Before I could think twice, I jumped to my feet and grabbed the guy by his gown. I had him down to the ground in a second pounding the tar out of him, as he tried to shield his face and head from my blows.

Staff came in and pulled me off the guy before I caused grave physical harm. By then, I came to my senses and calmed down. Immediately, I realized what I'd done and felt awful about it. They removed the guy from the room but let me stay after I apologized and promised it wouldn't happen again.

GROUP THERAPY DIDN'T AMOUNT TO MUCH. A middle-aged female therapist, with graying hair and shoes that squeaked slightly when she walked, led a small group of us in art therapy. The woman circled around the room, approaching each table with a mechanical grin that made me not trust her. She stared in feigned interest at the pictures or, in some cases, blank sheet of paper, asking questions: "What do we have here?" and "My, what is this about?" A few patients talked to her about their drawing or other matters, but most stared out blankly into space or scribbled on the page without any concern for her presence.

I sat with my blank page and untouched crayons and tried to avoid her attentions. Of course, she eventually found her way over to me and attempted to engage me in talk. I didn't have anything to say. By now, my head had cleared, and instead of working through my feelings with crayons, I was busy figuring out what I needed to do to get my affairs back in order.

I'd messed up. I retraced my four-day binge over and over in my mind, trying to figure the tally of my damage: who I'd "borrowed" money from for more booze and drugs, who I'd scammed or hustled and needed to avoid for a while, who I'd pissed off or hurt and needed to apologize to.

I knew I had plenty of fixing ahead of me. The first step, though, was making a new start. Just as I had a thousand times, I swore off cocaine. Of course, I reassured myself, I could drink. Drinking wasn't my problem; cocaine was my problem. Evil, demonic-inspired white powder was my problem, and I was done with that: no more, not again. Once the facility released me, I'd go to my mother's house in Keystone Heights and start fresh. Get a job roofing. My brother Billy lived there with Mom and Marion. She'd always told me I could stay with her if I needed. I just needed a few months to get my act together, stay off the needle, and work hard. Maybe get a place of my own. Settle down.

A few days ago, I'd been sitting in the middle of San Jose Boulevard. Broken. Crying and cursing. But, now, I had my wits about me. I felt better. Things would be better. Things *had* to be better.

The definition of insanity is doing the same
thing over and over and over and over again,
but expecting a different result.
ALBERT EINSTEIN

CHAPTER 14

From Bad to Worse

H OW DO YOU DO IT?"
"You smoke it, dude," Casey Harland said. Casey shook the pill bottle containing the crack cocaine. Something that sounded like pebbles rattled in the plastic bottle.

I'd never heard of crack. It was late 1987. Crack had been on the scene in big cities, especially in low-income neighborhoods, but new drugs took their time finding their way to small towns like Keystone Heights. In fact, back then, I couldn't find crack in Keystone—but I could in Starke, twelve miles north on State Road 100.

For now, I didn't need to locate a crack dealer. I had my friend Casey, a dealer with plenty of the new drug to share. I was heavy into my cocaine addiction, even after the Jacksonville Mental Health Resource Center released me from the 72-hour hold, and game for whatever might get me high and provide some release from my obsessions.

Casey took a hit from the crack pipe, then grabbed a pistol laying on his living room coffee table. I watched in half amusement, half horror as he ran to a closet in the front hallway. Positioning himself in the doorway of the open closet, he held the gun up, aligned with his broad shoulders, cocked and ready.

"Man, you hear that?" Casey exclaimed through clenched teeth. "Look out the front window! You see anybody?"

Casey had been a member of the Outlaws, an infamous biker gang. I wanted to laugh at his crazy antics, but didn't dare, not with Casey holding a loaded weapon. I didn't really think he'd turn on me—we'd been friends for years—but I was clear-headed enough not to take chances. I learned right then that crack cocaine induces paranoia.

The first time I smoked it—that night with Casey—crack did little for me. I was used to shooting dust into my veins. Crack was cheaper, but the high wasn't as good to me. I'd have to do more of it to get the same effect. Its low cost finally made scoring powder cocaine much harder, if not impossible, and even more expensive than before.

The first time I bought crack rock, on 8th Street in Jacksonville, was a lesson in frustration. I'd smoked it a few times with other users, Casey and others, but never had to deal directly with the substance. Like with shooting cocaine at first, I was clueless.

Feeling the obsession to use, I pulled up to a dealer in one of the downtown dope holes, hoping to find powder. Chances were slim, though. Everyone by this time was smoking crack. I was desperate and ready to take whatever I could get my hands on.

I gave the guy my money. He handed me two rocks. Down the road, I pulled over my truck and tried to break a rock down in the spoon I kept for shooting up. It wouldn't break down. I knew nothing of the process of making crack and didn't have a pipe like the one Casey used. I figured I'd just mash it up and shoot it into a vein, but it wouldn't break the way I wanted. Out of frustration and anger, I threw the rocks out the truck window.

A year later, I would have been on the ground rooting around for it.

AT LEAST WITH CRACK, I WAS OFF THE NEEDLE.
After a while, the track marks up and down my arms healed. My arms no longer constantly ached, but hitting the pipe seemed a new low for me. Just as I'd judged shooting up as some lower form of drug use—certainly, I couldn't be a junkie—smoking crack was something *real* addicts did, folks on the bottom of the drug-use scale. That wasn't me, I lied to myself. In

my mind, I was just smoking crack so I could hide the track marks from friends and family. In my warped way of thinking, I was somehow better than the crack addicts in the dope holes. It was a screwed-up way of rationalizing my addiction and kept me sick, but my disease had ahold of me and told me the lies to keep me going back for more.

I was living mostly in Keystone with my brother Billy and Mom. Mom's husband Marion and their two kids, Joel and Deana, were there as well, though we weren't close. I couldn't blame them for the distance between us. Anyone would have had a hard time staying close to me then. My addiction consumed my life. I tried to hide it from everyone as much as possible, but I'm sure they saw through me, that any interaction with them was only surface level and meant very little. What mattered to me more were alcohol and drugs. Even during the days that I looked perfectly fine, each day was a fight to maintain my sanity. I wasn't really living. I was living life in a blackout.

Even Mitch—whom I looked up to as a father figure of sorts and whom I trusted and admired—had no idea of the severity of my illness. I hardly talked to my father by that point, especially since Uncle David's death, which strangely I got the feeling he somehow blamed me for. Living in Keystone was a way to get out of the temptations of Sin City, but even living out in the country couldn't stop my addiction. The devil will find you—wherever you are.

THE SAYING GOES, "IF YOU ARE GOING THROUGH HELL, keep going." I'd been going through hell for years, and—against all sane judgment—I'd stopped.

Then again, maybe I hadn't. Maybe over the years, I'd kept going, only deeper into hell, instead of out. This period of my life felt like hell, the hell I created through my addiction and the consequences of my behaviors while feeding my addiction.

One particular bad choice that haunts me still today involved stealing money from my friend Fish.

Fish still lived in Starke. We'd stayed friends since our time in eighth grade together. From time to time, I stayed with Fish in his trailer, a few blocks from the easiest spot in Starke to buy crack cocaine.

At that point, I worked for a guy in Keystone, just on a daily basis, odd jobs making fifty dollars a day. Fish didn't do cocaine, but he did drink. I'd borrow Mom's old car after work and drive to Starke to hang out in the bar with Fish, drinking and shooting pool until my fifty bucks was gone. I'd have short periods when I'd try to stay off the pipe, but drinking would usually bring on the obsession. One night the compulsion got bad. Real bad. Bad enough to steal money out of Fish's wallet after he'd gone to bed. I'd have done anything at that point to get money for crack.

I spent the night using, smoking rock after rock, out in the woods of Starke, making it back to Keystone Heights around daybreak. The next morning, Fish called to tell me his money was missing. He blamed his brother-in-law, who'd been at the trailer as well. I hate that I allowed it to happen, but I let Fish believe his brother-in-law had stolen from him, even encouraging it. I felt guilty but played right along, feigning anger, agreeing that his brother-in-law had been the culprit, disgusted with myself for not having the guts to tell him the truth.

ON ANOTHER OCCASION DURING THIS SAME PERIOD, MY crack use nearly landed me in jail—and took off half my hind to boot.

State Road 100 that connects Keystone Heights and Starke is a rural stretch of road, populated by pine trees, potato and collards crops, and the occasional chicken farm, at least until you get into Starke's town limits. Just outside of the town, where South Water Street becomes State Road 100 and the CSX railroad tracks cut the road, a little bar used to sit off the road about 100 feet. At least it did in the late 1980s. It may be there still, but I've good reason not to revisit it.

As usual, I'd taken the money I'd earned for my day's labor and hitched a ride north on SR 100 into Starke to party with Fish and smoke crack until I'd blown through the cash in my pocket, which never took long. On that particular night, I'd spent my last nickel and run out of folks to ask for a loan, knowing fully I'd no intention to repay their generosity. As I walked SR 100 back toward Keystone Heights, I passed in front of the bar, closed in the dead of the night and waiting like a party invitation to open.

Being an experienced roofer, I'd no qualms about climbing up to the roof. The building had a pitched roof that made access and maneuver easy, although it could make detection from the road easy, too. Just as I had neglected to do at nineteen, parked behind Sonny's Bar-B-Q, I failed to think through my impulses all the way to their possible conclusions.

Finding a way in from the roof was simple. I spied the turbine ventilator right away. Positioned on the side of the roof that faced the road, the ventilator was in clear view for anyone passing by. The thought registered for a brief moment but then disappeared as I yanked the turbine's aluminum hood back and forth until the screws that held it gave way, exposing the twelve-inch hole that dropped down to the building's attic, which was no more than a two-foot crawlspace. I used my heavy work boots to my advantage and quickly kicked out the drop ceiling tile below the ventilator shaft. Everything was going fine. I'd crawl through the shaft, drop down into the bar, and help myself to whatever cash I could find. I had a few more hours until daylight and my addiction screamed for attention.

One of the side effects of stimulant use, such as crack, is a decrease in appetite. I'd lost considerable weight as my cocaine, then crack, addiction escalated, and I'd no doubt that I'd fit through the turbine shaft. I stripped off my T-shirt, now damp from the sweat of my activity. Without haste, I lowered myself into the open shaft, fitting my legs through with no problem. At my hips, the fit became snug, so I wiggled back and forth, squirming my way through the shaft. The sharp aluminum of the turbine sliced into my bare skin, but I didn't stop. At my waist, I stopped squirming.

I was stuck. The shaft was too small.

I tried not to panic as I considered what to do next. After a minute, I tried it again, sucking in my breath and contracting my stomach and chest muscles tight. I squirmed my way down another inch or so, but had to stop again. *Don't panic*, I told myself. Surely, with some maneuvering, I would squeeze the rest of the way through. This was just a minor setback.

And, I didn't panic . . . not until I saw the police car coming up SR 100.

The officer's headlights approached slowly. I wracked my brain for plausible explanations for being halfway through a turbine ventilator on the roof of a closed bar in the middle of the night. For once, I could think of no BS story that made sense. I was sure I was going to jail.

Then, I started to panic.

The squad car made its way up the road in what seemed like slow motion as I twisted violently back and forth, trying to will myself through the space. The sharp edge of the shaft sliced deeper into my flesh. Farther down my midsection, I felt the scraping of metal bolts across my skin. The bolts, meant to hold the lower and upper sections of the shaft together, were tiny daggers, stabbing me repeatedly as I fought for every centimeter of movement. The pain was excruciating, but I pushed it aside. I wouldn't let the cops catch me like this. Making it through the shaft was my only option.

When the squad car passed the building without its lightbar coming to life or a voice bellowing for me to *Freeze!*—as if I'd have any other choice—my heart stopped pounding. Apparently, the officer hadn't looked up. If he had, I'd have been clear enough to spot. For a moment, I thought luck was on my side, but then I remembered my predicament.

The police hadn't seen me, but I was still wedged into a turbine shaft, with its sharp aluminum edge making sliced beef of my body. I took a deep breath and focused my manic thoughts. I was too far in to push my way back out. Besides, there was still my addiction and probable cash in the register or office, and I needed my next fix more than ever. Having taken further stock of the situation, I once again took a deep breath, raised my arms, and contracted my muscles, inching my way down like a fiendish worm. I let out a muffled scream as I forced my way through the last few inches, falling onto the concrete floor.

For a moment, I lay a bloodied heap of flesh, unable to move, but I knew I'd no time to waste. For all I knew, maybe the cop had seen me and was just waiting for backup. The thought seemed ridiculous, but the whole situation was ridiculous—another stop on my journey through hell.

I got what cash was in the register—fifty bucks, maybe less—then made the horrific journey back through the shaft. Metal security bars covered the tavern's windows and doors, so no luck going out by easier means. This time through the ventilator shaft, though, the blood covering my torso helped to lubricate my body, making it easier to slide through.

I should have gone straight home. Of course, I didn't. Not until I'd walked back into Starke—cut to ribbons, a mangled, wretched creature—

to buy more crack. Back at Mom's house, I weaved a fantastic, harrowing story of having been hit by a car while crossing the parking lot of a convenience store. For a week, I lay in bed recovering, at first unable to stand and walk, lest the pain drop me back to the bed.

As soon as I could move, I went back to Starke for more.

By the time Mitch saw me several weeks later, most of the cuts and bruises had healed, except for some of the deepest slices under my arms and on my hands. Mitch bought the lie about the hit and run. Of course he did. My addiction gave me all the motivation I needed to be a master manipulator. I was adept at making others feel sorry for me, want to help me, enable me to continue in my addiction. Mitch had been there for me whenever I'd needed him. He was understanding and helpful, always quick to think the best of me.

I was about to test that relationship and place it foolishly at risk.

I'd gone to Jacksonville from Keystone Heights and Mom's house to visit with Mitch. We'd been drinking since he got off work that evening and it was late. Mitch offered me the couch for the night and went off to sleep. As it had been all along, once I started drinking the urge to use the drug of my choice, which at this time was crack, came over me like an inescapable nightmare.

Mitch lived in Jacksonville Beach, and I knew I could score crack in an area of south Jax Beach called "The Hill." Unfortunately, Mitch's house was a ways from the Hill. The urge to use was strong, and I knew the quickest way to find what I needed was to take Mitch's car.

Mitch loved his black 1986 Caprice Classic. It was like his baby, his pride and joy, and I knew it. In my addictive mind, I rationalized that I would just borrow the Caprice to run up to the Hill. I wouldn't be but a short time. Besides, Mitch had laid the keys on the coffee table. They were there for me to take. Obviously, I told myself, Mitch would want to help me out. He always had before. I'd just be a few minutes.

Really.

Once I used, nothing could've stopped me. I was revved up and ready. The next three days, I did whatever it took to find the ways and means to keep using, not considering what it would mean to Mitch that I'd taken his car without his permission. I hit every dope hole I knew in Jacksonville, smoking crack and drinking, but mostly smoking all the crack I could get my hands on. My mental state was such that I was lost in my addiction, the insanity and need in me so great that consequences didn't matter, relationships didn't matter, nothing mattered except that next high. My appetite for drugs was insatiable. I was an empty hole that could not be filled.

By the end of the third day, I was exhausted and out of means to keep using. Even if I'd had a way, my body could take no more. I'd punished and abused it to the point that I was physically ill and psychologically broken.

Yet, some kernel of sanity remained, however small, and I knew I needed help. I'd taken Mitch's car and couldn't simply drive it back and confess that I was addicted to crack and couldn't stop. I couldn't go to Grandma White's house and have her discover the wretch I'd become. Even going back to my mother's house in Keystone Heights seemed out of the question. I'd enough sense to know I'd only return to Starke and buy more crack the minute I could get a few bucks in my pocket. In that miserable state, I knew of nothing else to do or anywhere else to go— except back to where I'd gone before when coming so close to the edge.

I called Mitch from the Mental Health Resource Center and told him he'd find his car parked behind MHRC. For all my distraught feelings about being committed to the facility and my promises to stop using cocaine, I'd escalated in my addiction to smoking crack, stolen from my friends, broken into private property, and angered and disappointed the man I looked to as a father figure. My addictive mind had led me to a place I'd vowed never to return.

I was in *the cuckoo's nest*.

Again.

If you are going through hell,
keep going.
WINSTON CHURCHILL

CHAPTER 15
Sick and Tired

I SPENT THREE DAYS IN MHRC, GOING THROUGH the same rounds as before: intake, evaluation, group therapy, release. The Jacksonville Mental Health Resource Center hadn't changed.

But, I had.

I hadn't meant to steal Mitch's car. I'd no intent to cause him pain. Once started, though, I'd locked away all thoughts of consequences and feelings and loyalties. Nothing had been as important as keeping the madness going. I realized I'd come to a place where I could no longer hide my addiction in the easy manner I had for so long. My efforts to minimize no longer worked. My cover was blown.

I had two options: get help or run from the problem.

I'd gone to the place I thought would offer help, and it had been no help. So, I chose the second route.

I left MHRC and headed back to Keystone Heights. At least, I figured, I'd gotten a few days rest to regroup. My addiction had not disappeared, though I told myself—for the thousandth time—I'd make a real effort to stay off my drug of choice.

Back in Keystone Heights, my addiction picked up just where it had left off, even stronger now. Laughing in my face. Who was I to make promises to leave it behind? What was I but a pitiful creature, slave to its demands?

What I needed, I rationed, was to be smarter, more clever, more secretive. I needed steadier work to make money to use and a place to stay by myself, so I could isolate and use without having to go off into the woods or lay up in crack houses. If I had any chance of keeping my addiction hidden from others, or at least less in their faces, I needed to live on my own.

I found an answer to both these issues—employment and a place to live—in the generosity and kindness of man named John who owned a roofing company in Keystone Heights. John hired me to roof for his company and rented a cabin in Keystone to me. Like Mitch, John was a gentle soul who saw the good in me. As was also with Mitch, I'd do all I could to destroy his trust. My addiction would see to that.

I didn't intend to break into John's house. I never intended to do most of the bad things I did—at least at this point. I'd go to his house late at night, already tapped out of my own funds, ready with a hundred excuses about why I needed money and with one aim in mind: to continue using. On one such occasion, I found him away from home. Jonesing for my next fix, I broke into his house.

I didn't go in with the thought of stealing a check. I just needed some money, maybe twenty dollars. Enough to buy more crack and get me though the night. There his checkbook lay, just an opportunity to be seized. I tore out a check, filled it out in my name, and signed John's name to it. Down the road was a store where I knew I could cash it. Everyone there knew me and John, had seen us together a number of times. I knew no one would hassle me about it. I pocketed the hundred and fifty dollars and hightailed it back to Starke.

In the back of my mind, I knew I'd get caught. Here again, like stealing Mitch's car, I'd set myself up to exposure. Stealing from John with a forged check made out in my name, cashed in front of people who knew me. What was I thinking? I wasn't thinking. Or, maybe I was trying to get caught, subconsciously seeking a way to stop the chaos. After smoking crack until dawn, I returned home. Immediately, I fell into a deep, dark depression. How could I do such a thing to this good man who'd tried to help me? I'd really screwed up this time.

I knew I couldn't go back to work and face John. Like a coward, I retreated, locking myself in my cabin. I shut the curtains and kept off the lights. When anyone would knock at the door, I'd pretend not to be home. I wished for a hole to hide in, so miserable was my state of mind. Finally, after three days, I went to John and confessed . . . partially. I told him I'd cashed the check but that I'd found it in his truck, while on the job site. I never told him I broke into his home. Tears in my eyes, I begged for his forgiveness, promising to pay the money back or to work it off. In my mind, taking the check from his work truck was better than climbing through his living room window.

John said he forgave me, but I couldn't forgive myself. Soon after the incident, I left the job with John and the little cabin and returned to Jacksonville. I'd disappointed John. I'd disgusted myself. In my mind, there was one place a miserable creature like me could feel a measure of warmth, but I'd have to return home.

AT LEAST MOVING IN WITH GRANDMA WHITE MEANT I could be close to her. We'd still kept in touch, but she'd no idea of my pain and suffering; hiding my illness was perhaps easiest, and hardest, with her.

I was sick, but I'd been so good at covering up my addiction. If you'd put me in a lineup and asked ten people to pick the guy that looked like a clean, stand-up fellow, they would've picked me. Still, Grandma could tell something was wrong. Eventually, after a drug binge, I broke down and told Grandma I needed help—of course, still trying to minimize the severity of my disease. I just needed a rest, a reprieve. I admitted to my grandmother that I was using drugs, but I wasn't willing to admit fully my addiction.

Grandma White found my first Twelve-Step meeting, off Cassat Avenue, across the St. Johns River. I'd bought a little junk car and promised her I'd go. A few beers beforehand helped muster up the nerve to walk through the doors. The meeting already in progress, I took a seat in the back of the room, avoiding eye contact. A man read from a sheet of paper, something about "Steps." The sayings and readings continued, all foreign-sounding to me. For all I comprehended, they might as well have been speaking Swahili.

After the readings, a man got up and stood at a podium. He told his story of drug addiction: how it had destroyed his life and how he'd found strength and hope in recovery. At one point, he choked back tears. I squirmed in my chair, the room seemingly smaller than when I'd walked in. This wasn't what I'd imagined: folks talking gibberish about "Steps" and "Traditions," men crying about the years they'd wasted stoned and strung out. Honestly, I didn't know what I'd imagined a Twelve-Step meeting to be—but not like this.

I left before the guy at the podium finished his speech.

When Grandma asked about the meeting, I told her I thought it had been real helpful and that I was looking forward to the next one. There wasn't a next one for me, not then. In an attempt to continue my denial, I told Grandma I was attending meetings. Eventually, my phantom meetings became a good excuse to leave the house and convenient way to cover my tracks. I felt lucky to have found them. Now I could go on using. Grandma knew I was sick, but I was getting help.

The day I committed strong-arm robbery, Grandma thought I was at a meeting.

HANK G. WAS A GUY FROM THE NEIGHBORHOOD, BACK IN Sin City. In fact, I'd been introduced to him through Julie, after the two started snorting coke in the nightclubs of Jacksonville, while I was locked up for the Sonny's Bar-B-Q break-in. It was Hank's idea to rob someone outside of Winn Dixie on Arlington Road. We'd wait outside the grocery store for a woman to enter, then snatch her purse. We'd buy our drugs and split whatever remained, which we knew would probably be nothing. Hank didn't have a car, so we'd have to use mine. We also decided I'd do the snatching and Hank would be the driver.

That was it, our big plan.

Hank pulled along Arlington Road, leaving the car running, while I stood outside the grocery store. An older lady, maybe in her midfifties, approached the store doors. As she passed, I reached out and yanked her purse out of her hands, then shot out toward Hank and the parked car.

In my eagerness to snatch the bag, I hadn't noticed the two big guys on the other end of the store entrance. When I grabbed the woman's purse, the two of them took after me, chasing me across the parking lot. At the car, I threw the bag through the open passenger-side window. Still in chase, the guys must have spooked Hank because he didn't wait for me to open the passenger door. Instead, he peeled away from the shoulder and sped away.

Not knowing what else to do, I ran into the woods alongside the road, the two men still following. It was nighttime and pitch black. I stopped running and lay on the hard ground. In the darkness, I could see nothing, but I could hear the men talking near the side of the road. After a while they left.

Thinking to avoid the men and, I worried, likely the police, I made my way farther into the woods. I figured I'd avoid the main roads. In the dark, I misjudged my exact location and shortly ended up in a swampy portion of land near Silversmith Creek. It wasn't long walking before I found myself up to my neck in swamp water. In the dark, I trudged through the muck, eventually spilling out into the Glenlea neighborhood of Arlington. By the time I got back to Hank's house an hour and a half later, Hank had forty dollars left. I don't know if he'd already used without me, but I would imagine he did.

I probably would have.

Covered in mud and leaves, cold and miserable, my big payoff was a lousy twenty bucks. I spent the rest of the night getting high and trying to forget the stupid act I'd committed just to feed my addiction. If I could get high enough, I could forget and tomorrow would be a better day. Tomorrow, I'd stop all this chaos. Tomorrow, I'd put the past behind me.

If only wishes and empty promises made it so. Tomorrow came and a new reality sank in.

No master criminals, Hank and I hadn't thought to take the tag off my car. One of the guys had recorded the tag number. The police had gone to my grandma's apartment already looking for me. People I knew in Sin City told me the cops had been asking about me. It was only a matter of time.

The robbery occurred May 6, 1989. The following weeks were hell. I wanted only two things: to hide from the reality of what I'd done and to use. My thoughts raced, trying to figure out my next move. I knew I'd really messed up. I smoked crack almost continuously, sure that the police were hot on my trail.

After three weeks bingeing and ducking my usual hangouts, afraid a cop might catch notice of me, I pushed a shopping cart around the Publix Super Market along Arlington Expressway, not far from where I'd snatched the lady's purse. I'd gone without food for several days and needed just enough to keep me on my feet. This wasn't my first time lifting food from a grocery store. I'd push the cart around, grabbing a quart of chocolate milk and a hotdog or sandwich from the deli, and eat while pretending to shop. After eating two hotdogs and drinking a full quart of milk, I abandoned the shopping cart in the middle of a grocery aisle.

Outside the Publix, I slumped down against the storefront, next to a set of pay phones. I hadn't slept in days, and the food on my stomach made me drowsy. I closed my eyes, just wanting to rest awhile.

The shouts of teenage voices brought me back sharply to where I was.

"How you doing, you friggin' bum?"

"Go get a job, loser!"

A carload of teens passed slowly in front of me. I tried getting to my feet as their taunts and laughter continued.

The reality of my condition crashed into me with each verbal assault. They were right. I was a bum, a loser. I deserved their ridicule. I was worthless.

In my desperation, the only thing I could think to do was to turn myself in. I leaned up against the pay phone as I called the police department, determined to report myself for strong-arm robbery. I wouldn't give up Hank, but I'd tell them I'd stolen a woman's purse and they'd take me to jail, where maybe I'd get the help I needed to get straight. I needed to be punished. I needed to pay for the miserable creature I'd become.

The female officer that responded to dispatch's call, an attractive, young blonde, must have had a hard time understanding my incoherent ramblings. I tried explaining that I'd committed a crime. The cops knew exactly what I'd done, I professed, and she needed to take me in for my crime. Apparently, a warrant for the burglary had not been issued yet. Instead of taking me to jail, she dropped me off in an all-too familiar place: the Mental Health Resource Center. I was back at MHRC for the third, and final, time.

This go-around the facility had the good sense to inform me they could do nothing for me. I had a drug and alcohol problem, as they explained it, not a mental illness. After a couple of phone calls, they placed me in a cab for detox. I remember thinking maybe *this* was the hope for me, the magic solution. Detox would get me clean. I could get back on my feet.

Like the first Twelve-Step meeting, I didn't know what to expect, but I knew I was running out of options. I had to be put somewhere. I needed shelter from the storm.

I'D HEARD ABOUT THE DETOX A FEW TIMES. IN MY MIND, I imagined a big, square room with hard metal cots lined against stark white walls. The floor of the room slanted down to a center drain that caught urine, or vomit, or whatever else might spill to the vinyl tiles and need washing away. The image was disturbing, but I was willing to go to whatever lengths this time to turn my life around. I had nowhere else to go.

Detox, in downtown Jacksonville, turned out to be more like a well-secured office building than anything I imagined. A professionally dressed, polite black man with neat braids buzzed me into the admissions office and helped me fill out the necessary paperwork. A nurse took my vital signs, recorded my drug use, and explained the detox process. I was tired but tried to answer her questions as completely and honestly as possible. After a while, I was given a bed and quickly drifted off to sleep, only to be woken up every four hours for more taking of vital signs and to receive a shot in the rear end; of what, I still don't know.

After three days, a caseworker called me into his office.

The caseworker propped his elbows onto his desk, leaned forward, and asked, "Mr. White, what do you want to do?"

His question took me aback. "What do you mean?"

"I mean, what do you want to do?"

I couldn't remember if I'd ever been asked so directly what I wanted, about my substance use or anything in life. For a moment, all I could do was stare into his big, brown eyes. Eyes that seemed to care what I wanted and needed.

I tried to answer, stammering, thrown by his directness. "I don't . . . don't get what . . . what do you mean?"

He repeated the question a third time, louder, emphasizing each word. *"What do you want to do, Mr. White?"*

I broke down. Years of frustration, guilt, and shame rose like a flood tide. "Man, I want to quit doing this! I want to quit, and I can't!"

His voice softened. "Are you willing to go to treatment?"

I remember when he asked me that question he might as well have asked, *Would you like me to give you a million bucks?* He was giving me more than a million dollars, more than riches. He was offering me the yellow brick road, the way into Oz. In my mind, he was offering me *the cure.*

Here it was at last. Someone would fix me.

Peace comes from within.
Do not seek it without.
BUDDHA

CHAPTER 16

The Fix: June 1989

T REATMENT MEANT YOU GOT FIXED.

I was willing to stay in detox until a bed opened up at the Gateway Community Services treatment center—however long it took.

It turned out to take thirty days. During that time, staff moved me from the temporary detox area to a nicer wing of the building that housed other men and women waiting for a treatment bed.

Treatment was the secret that life had hidden from me for so long. Each day meant a day closer to learning the secret, and I was ready to hear it, ready to absorb it all and let it work its magic. I hadn't yet learned that treatment wasn't a magic pill. I didn't understand I had a living problem. I didn't know how to cope with life. No one was going to *fix* me.

The day after the caseworker offered to send me to Gateway, I tore the ligaments in my ankle playing basketball on the courts reserved for the chosen "treatment-bound" patients. I spent the thirty days hobbling on crutches, smoking cigarettes, and attending pretreatment sessions led by two counselors, a male and a female. Recovering addicts themselves, they tried to prepare us the best they could for what we'd soon face. I read all the pamphlets and literature: again, running into phrases like *The Twelve Steps* and *The Twelve Traditions*. This time, they made a little more sense.

I could understand there was something I needed to do to turn my life around, something for which I was accountable.

Eventually, a bed opened up for me at Gateway. I felt beyond ready to take the next step. Walking into the facilities felt like I imagined it would—a burden seemed lifted from me. The facility had a swimming pool, good food, and plenty of folks eager to listen. I could have lived there forever.

Some of the folks in treatment, though, seemed eager to do their time and leave. Those that wanted the most to leave sounded as if they had lives outside the facility worth going back to. I felt I had nothing waiting for me outside the treatment walls. In fact, the only thing that seemed waiting for me was the law. I figured at some point what I'd tried to explain to the pretty, blonde officer who'd picked me up and driven me to MHRC would catch up to me. I might as well enjoy myself while I could.

I was a model treatment patient my first time at Gateway. I went to Twelve-Step meetings and did whatever they told me to do, making a point to be friendly with the workers and counselors. Soon, everyone knew and liked me.

Like a chameleon, within a few weeks I spoke the language, could quote the literature, and knew just what to say so all those around me were certain I'd make a full recovery. In fact, a survey or superlatives list of some kind circulated around the facility, at some point, and staff voted me "Most Likely to Succeed" in recovery. I believed it, too. I wanted to be in recovery, to get clean. Two weeks before graduation from treatment, the cops showed up to arrest me on the warrant for strong-arm robbery.

The day they came for me, I was lifting weights in the yard. I'd been a wreck when I'd entered detox, but by this time, I was clean, taking care of my body, and bulking up. As I curled the hand weights, head slightly down, from the corner of my eye, I caught a glimpse of the detective's shiny black shoes.

The detective put his hand on my arm.

I lowered the weights. The gig was up.

"Timothy White?" the detective holding my arm asked.

"Yes." I didn't try to lie. What good would it have done?

"Come with us. We need to talk."

140

The second detective followed silently behind us as we entered the facility and into the cafeteria. I could tell the detectives didn't enjoy having to pull me out of treatment. They were respectful and kind, and, though they had to handcuff me, allowed me to return to my room for my possessions, including recovery literature to read while in jail. As we passed back through the yard, I heard other treatment clients yell, "Don't take him away!" and "Leave him alone!"

The judge set bond at fifty thousand dollars. After a few weeks, the judge held a bond reduction hearing and lowered the amount to twenty-five thousand. Somehow, my family scraped money together for the bond, and the court released me to the treatment center.

Mitch drove me straight back to Gateway.

Graduation from treatment—at that point—was the happiest day of my life. When I proceeded across the stage to receive my certificate, Mom, Billy, Mark, and Mitch clapped loudly. I thanked everyone for believing in my success. I'd earnestly completed all the paperwork and gone through the motions in just the way expected. I felt cured. After the ceremony, Mom hugged me tight. Mitch and my brothers shook my hand and slapped me on the back. In my mind, I'd made good.

I was starting over.

Mitch let me set up a travel trailer next to his house, and it wasn't long before I found work roofing. On a one-year house arrest, the courts allowed me to go to work, make Twelve-Step meetings, check in with my probation officer, and attend church. Also, I could go back to school for my GED, so I signed up for classes at the local junior college—more for somewhere to go than to further my education.

Though I was making it, doing all the right things—or so I thought—I felt alienated from the life I'd always known. I didn't want to be an addict. I wanted to be normal, and normal to me was drinking, hanging out at clubs, going to parties. That lifestyle still felt a part of me. I resented being ostracized from it and the life I'd always known. It wasn't fair that everyone else got to drink, and I didn't. I'd done my time in treatment and graduated. I had the certificate and pats on the back. Why wasn't that enough? Why couldn't I enjoy myself the way I wanted?

In my self-denial, I couldn't see the obvious answers.

After six months, I began testing myself.

In my mind, if I stayed off cocaine, in whatever form the drug came, everything else would be acceptable to me. I reasoned that it would be fine for me to go to a bar and have a drink or two. Unwind. I deserved it, didn't I, for all my hard work since leaving treatment? Even the thought of being completely drug free—no mood or mind-altering substances of any kind—seemed ridiculous. I couldn't live like that. How did a person live that way?

It started with trips to a restaurant and bar, Calico Jack's, where I'd been a regular before detox and Gateway. I'd go straight there after my Twelve-Step meeting. The first night back at the bar, I drank a White Russian, trying to sip it, make it last, then downing it in one gulp. The first drink went down easily, then the second. After the third, I'd proven to myself that I wasn't an addict. I could drink and be fine. I drove home certain that as long as I stayed away from crack, alcohol wasn't problematic for me.

The next week, I went to Calico Jack's a second time.

Again, I had three or four drinks, just enough to catch a buzz and get right. I left before I consumed enough vodka to feel drunk, feeling pleased with myself that I'd figured this addiction deal out. I was right: alcohol wasn't the problem, cocaine was.

I left Calico Jack's the third time and headed straight for a crack dealer.

ONCE I DRANK, I WAS GONE. THOUGH IN REALITY, MY relapse began long before stepping foot back into a bar. When I began to feel sorry for myself and what I thought I was missing out on, when I assured myself that I deserved a drink for the good progress I was making, that's when the relapse began. My relapse started with my diseased thinking. Putting a drink in my hand just made the next steps come quicker. Drinking made it acceptable for me to turn to my drug of choice: crack. If I were sober, I remained strong enough to fight back the obsessions. I still had a chance at working through my destructive thoughts. I could have gone to more meetings. I could have called my sponsor. I chose to do neither of those things.

Once I picked up a drink, I was powerless against my addiction. The demon had hold of me again; my descent was lightening quick. That third night back to the bar was all it took. I found myself leaving Calico Jack's and driving toward downtown Jacksonville, to Florida Avenue where I could score easily, almost as if I were a plane on automatic pilot—set for crash.

By that time, I'd left the trailer at Mitch's house. My brother Billy and I had rented an apartment at the beach. Still on house arrest, I'd only enough time to make the meeting and drive home with a few minutes leeway between approved locations. So far, luck had been on my side. No probation officer had stopped in to check on me after the meeting.

That night, my luck ran out.

By the time I got home from my drug run, including stopping to use, a community control officer had checked the apartment to verify my whereabouts and discovered me unaccounted for. I'd violated the conditions of my house arrest.

I panicked. There was no way I wasn't headed straight for jail, then prison. I grabbed a box of blank checks I'd acquired after recently opening a checking account. Billy tried to stop me from leaving. I pushed him aside.

With a bag full of clothes and the checks, I headed to Sin City—back to the familiar, though insane, life I'd always known. As expected, the neighborhood was the same, a den of drug use and dysfunction frozen in time. It waited for me with open arms, as did my addiction, which had only grown stronger.

Within days, I was broke. I sold the pickup I'd bought after leaving treatment. It brought in four hundred dollars, which paid for a rental car from an auto pawn business and more crack and booze.

After that cash ran dry, I started in on the blank checks, writing hot drafts until the box lay empty, consumed like a burned-out building.

My scams were numerous. I took orders for meat from folks around the neighborhood, then used checks to fill the orders from local butchers, selling the food at an irresistible discount. What did I care? It was free cash to buy more drugs. I'd write checks for boxes of Air Jordans, then trade the popular basketball shoes to drug dealers for product.

It went on like this for six weeks.

Around the end of May—almost a year from when I'd entered Gateway Community Services for alcohol and drug treatment—a police officer pulled me over, on Lamson Street, in the rented car I'd neglected to return to the auto pawn business two weeks prior. Some guy that I'd met at a drug dealer's house sat on the passenger side of the car. Before the cop made it to the driver-side window, I hid the remainder of the crack rock I had on me under my tongue.

Lamson Street cuts through the east end of Sin City, off Atlantic Boulevard. The guy beside me had no idea what I was about to do. From the rearview mirror, I watched the city squad car's lights swirl and the large, muscular officer—right hand on his gun, left hand shining his flashlight our way—advance toward us.

The car still in drive, I called out the open window, "What's the problem, officer?"

Just as he reached my window, I laid on the gas. The guy beside me gasped and grabbed hold of the bucket seat.

Behind us, I heard the police siren scream into the night. I took a sharp right onto Berry Avenue, a straight shot to Arlington Road and out to Atlantic Boulevard.

I drove like a madman down Berry, making it several blocks before I realized that outrunning the cop was probably not my best option.

My hand on the car door latch, I turned to the guy beside me, who was still grabbing hold of his seat, and yelled, "*Jump!*"

I hit the road and rolled. With a crash of metal and glass, the car careened into something, but I didn't stop to look. Once to my feet, I took off running, knowing that a dozen squad cars were headed our way.

My heart thumped in my chest as I ran through the streets and yards of Sin City, crack rock still under my tongue. Like a track and field athlete, I jumped a chain-linked fence, landing in some stranger's backyard. Sirens signaled the approach of police cars.

To my left sat a child's plastic pool. I rushed to the pool, which was no more than five feet in diameter, dropped to my knees, and curled up into the fetal position. Knees to my chest, I pulled the pool over me. My heart pounded in my ears. Panting, I tried to calm myself. As my breathing slowed, I realized the crack rock had numbed my entire mouth.

I waited in the dark—sure at any moment the cops would pull back my flimsy cover and shove their guns into my face. After a while, the sirens ceased. I threw off the pool and looked around. I wasn't sure they'd given up searching for me—in fact, I was convinced they hadn't—but they'd at least moved down the road. I saw no one.

Nearby was a dive called The Neighborhood Tavern. Panicked, I ran toward the Tavern, climbed onto its flat roof, and lay down. The sound of a helicopter whirled somewhere nearby. In the moist late-spring night, I lay as flat as I could against the roof, bits of gravel cutting into my cheeks, my sweat-drenched shirt cooling in the night air, sticking uncomfortably to my body. The familiar smell of tar filled my lungs as I lay listening for the copter and police sirens and trying to figure what to do next.

Eventually, the whirl of the helicopter passed. I climbed down from the roof and ran to a crack dealer's house, a different dealer than the one with whom I'd begun the evening. Too nervous to return to the first dealer's place, I beat it to a different dope hole. That night, I considered myself lucky to have dodged the cops. I marveled at my own quick thinking.

I don't know whatever happened to the unfortunate guy who was with me.

The next morning, in a car I'd borrowed from the dealer's girlfriend, I drove to Outrigger Apartments, a known drug location. This time, I took a guy named Freddy, another drug-user friend, along for the ride.

Only one road led in and out of the apartments, which made being there all the riskier. As we entered the complex, the police pulled us over.

Slowly, an officer approached the car. I glanced at his face and muscular arms. I couldn't believe it. It was the cop from the night before.

I remained calm. At first, he didn't recognize me.

I gave the officer my brother's name, Mark Boston, instead of my own. Not thinking clearly—having barely slept for days—I got Mark's birth date wrong by a day, a mistake that wouldn't catch up to me until I was sitting in jail.

After I gave my brother's name and the wrong birth date, the cop finally recognized me and said, "You're that guy from last night that ran on me."

I tried to argue. "I don't know what you're talking about. I didn't run from you."

He didn't buy it. The cop ordered me from the car and handcuffed me. Freddy, he told to hit the road. Freddy immediately obliged.

As the officer drove away from the apartments, out the only road to the main thoroughfare, I spied the dealer's girlfriend walking down the road, headed toward the apartment complex. I suppose we'd been gone too long. She'd come looking for us.

I remember the look of confusion on her face. She watched me pass as I sat helpless in the squad car's backseat. Brow furrowed, she held up her hands as if to say, *What the hell?*

I gave her a crooked smile.

I wasn't smiling inside, though. My luck had run out, and the fix that was rehab hadn't worked. I was still broken. And, now, I was off to prison.

Endure hardship as discipline; God is treating you as sons. For what son is not disciplined by his father?

HEBREWS 12:7

CHAPTER 17
Lock Up

THE JUDGE HANDED DOWN THE SENTENCE SWIFTLY: twenty-two months in the Florida State Prison system. No explanations on my part of how I could do better. No second chances—*or third or fourth*. No drug and alcohol treatment center. I'd reached the end of the road as far as the law was concerned.

On June 8, 1990, the road ended behind prison bars.

I'd disappointed everyone who'd ever cared for me. How I'd managed to successfully complete treatment, turn my life around, and then end up on a bus bound for the Lake Butler Florida Department of Corrections Reception and Medical Center baffled me.

The nearest I could figure, I was like Dr. Jekell and Mr. Hyde. When I wasn't using, I seemed like any other stand-up guy. Calm. Rational. When I fed my addiction, Mr. Hyde emerged, and I'd no defense against him or the havoc he wrecked. Dr. Jekell was sitting on the bus to Lake Butler, paying for Mr. Hyde's crimes.

I deserved the punishment, though. I was a worthless human being—subhuman even, as worthless as the rubber checks I'd bounced all over town. So far, the authorities hadn't brought up check-fraud charges. Of course, neither had I. I figured I'd no reason to continue to suffer for what Mr. Hyde had done during his drug-fueled tear.

I sat in the bus headed for the prison reception center, dressed in my street clothes and brandishing my "Rolex," the blue and orange double band that labeled those soon to be transported to state incarceration. No one spoke. Most of the inmates cast their eyes down, stared straight ahead, or watched out the windows at passing cars, as the distance between them and their freedom widened. Wherever they looked, they didn't look at one another.

Anxiety sat in the back of my throat like a bitter pill. I wondered if the other dozen or so men on the bus were as anxious as I. Were they worried about serving time? Going to jail, city lock up, was commonplace, almost a rite of passage; prison time, hard time, was a whole other situation. Some of the men were likely going away for life, and that was no joke.

The sound of the iron gate closing behind the bus echoed in my ears. As the bus doors opened, guards on and off the bus yelled at us to move out. Outside, guards with high-powered rifles kept their sights on us as we exited, one by one, and shuffled through a large, metal rollup door and into a warehouse that reminded me of a slaughterhouse with its pens and corrals, leading us to our eventual end. I held a bag of personal effects close as I stood in line, shoulder to shoulder, inside the large, empty space.

A baldheaded, no-neck correctional officer yelled at us, practically spitting. "You are now the property of the Florida State Prison!"

No one flinched. I looked down, avoiding eye contact with the officer.

He continued his tirade. "You will do what you're told to do, when you're told to do it!"

Inmates in white uniforms laid empty cardboard boxes at our feet. These inmates, referred to as "permanents," served out their time at the reception and medical center. I remember thinking how awful a punishment to be a permanent, to lay the two-foot square cardboard boxes at the feet of newly arrived prisoners month after month, year after year.

"You will now take your clothes off of your body!" No-Neck shouted. "You will deposit your clothes in the box provided to you!"

We striped down and placed our clothes and shoes in the box. Upon further instruction from No-Neck, we turned around and put our hands against the cold wall. As an officer made his way behind us, one-by-one we spread our buttocks for examination of contraband or weapons.

After the inspection, they led us through a series of reception rooms where we were issued temporary prison garb, assigned a number, and got our pictures taken, herded like cattle up a loading chute. In the span of a few minutes, I was transformed into number 280725.

At the end of the processing line, a permanent handed me a pair of black brogans, bedroll, blanket, and pillow. All that was left was our dorm assignment. I'd heard if the dorms were full, you might be assigned to a cellblock. You didn't want to be assigned to cellblock.

Of course, I was assigned to a cellblock. Cell 3B.

Cellblock is like a prison within a prison. Everything is different. Dark and dingy, cellblock offered none of the distractions allowed in the dorms, including no television. Its function was to house inmates on disciplinary lock down. Cellblock had a separate set of rules and a stricter means of operating, not to mention inmates who'd committed infractions or crimes since incarceration, offenses worthy of assignment into cellblock in the first place.

My anxiety increased as I walked the distance from the reception unit to the three-story cellblock building. With each step, my heart pounded faster, my muscles tightening into a fight-or-flight response. But I couldn't run. I glanced again at the guards with the high-powered rifles. No, I most certainly couldn't run this time.

Cellblock smelled of mold and the staleness of body odor. As I entered with my bedroll and pillow cradled in my arms, I looked up at the three tiers of cells within the open space. I would be on the second level. The eerie quiet of the unit played on my nerves even more. My boots clanged against the metal stairs as I ascended to level B. As the bars shut, I wondered how I'd survive in prison, promising myself again that after my release I'd stay far, far away from the life that had led me here.

I laid out my bedroll behind the metal bars of 3B and sat on the edge of my cell bed until time for lights out.

Lying in the darkness, the prison bed digging in my shoulder blades, I wondered again how I'd managed to mess up my life so utterly. From somewhere on level B, a guard shouted in a deep, grumbling voice. "I don't know who you people pray to, who your god is, but tonight, thank your god that I'm going home!"

I'd no idea who the guard was, but from the tone of his voice, I was indeed thankful he was going home.

I wished I were.

AFTER A WEEK AT LAKE BUTLER, A GUARD HANDED DOWN the awful news: I'd been made a permanent. The facility was building a new wing; with my construction background, officials flagged me to stay at Lake Butler to work the construction crew. Permanents on construction woke at 5:00 A.M. and worked grueling, miserable duty all day. Guards collected my blue temporary inmate garb and ordered me to change into the white uniform of a permanent.

The moment I learned the news, I started wracking my brain for a way out. I didn't want the laborious work detail of the construction crew. My mind flashed to images of chain-gang movies, prisoners chained to one another, slinging picks in the hot sun. I was still looking for an easy way out of my problems, a way to express my own self-will and to control my surroundings. I had to do something to escape this unfortunate turn of events.

On the advice of another inmate, I hatched the bright idea to declare a medical emergency. As explained by the inmate, if I claimed wanting to kill myself, the guards had to remove me from the permanents' list.

That was my out.

I marched up to the cellblock guard. "I declare a medical emergency."

The guard took me to the unit doctor.

The doctor looked me over and asked, "Do you ever think of suicide?"

"Constantly," I said.

Right away, the guards directed me to remove the white uniform. Once again, I was in the temp blues. A weight of desperation lifted off my shoulders. What I hadn't figured on is what events my statement had put into action. Inmates who threaten to kill themselves or, as I had, confess to suicidal thoughts, don't go to regular prison facilities. I was put on close custody and given Sinequan, the brand name for doxepin, a psychotropic agent.

Now, I'd really stepped into it.

Under the effect of Sinequan, I struggled to stay alert. My anxiety escalated, and I felt vulnerable. In prison, the last thing you want is others sensing your vulnerability and fear. I worried not only about violence at the hands of other inmates but from the guards as well. I'd heard stories of guards who beat prisoners who refused to follow orders to their liking or just to show their power over the inmates. Supposedly, a guard nicknamed K-Wing Slim kept a jar of inmates' teeth, like sick trophies.

Now I was a psych inmate. As was my pattern in my addiction, I'd failed to consider the consequences of my actions. I'd manipulated the system to avoid one set of circumstances, just to have a worse set thrust upon me. Obviously, sentencing me to prison had yet to result in a new way of thinking.

Officials transferred me from Lake Butler to Apalachee Correctional Institute in Sneads Florida, situated in the northern-central Florida Panhandle. Correctional officers came for me in the middle of the night, shackling me, the restraints locked at the waist with a black box. A C.O. shoved me into a transport van, and for the next several hours, I sat in silence, awaiting my fate.

By morning, we'd reached the facility. No one had told me where I was being transferred. I learned my location from a sign outside the prison gates. ACI was reserved for inmates on close custody, lifers, and murderers with "Buck Rogers" dates—end-of-sentence dates way, way in the future. Dread filled every pore of my body, spread to every nerve. Once again, imposing my own self-will had led me down a worse path.

After processing, I carried my bedroll across the compound. ACI looked worlds different from Lake Butler. Clothesline hung across dorms. Prisoners walked the center courtyard. The prison resembled a little city. Inside the dorm, inmates lounged around shirtless. A young, white boy braided an older black man's hair, the boy's pant leg rolled up to reveal a pink sock. I gathered that the young boy was the older man's "girlfriend."

I didn't see a guard in sight.

Again, I wondered what I'd gotten myself into. Why did I always manage to make my situation worse? The cellblock at Lake Butler had felt like prison. I didn't know what to make of this place.

In my new environment, I quickly learned the system. I was assigned as a houseman, which meant I had to mop the dorm floors for several hours a day. To avoid hassle from other inmates, I adopted a stance and posture that communicated I was not to be messed with. I suppose, considering the circumstances, being labeled mentally unstable was a benefit. If anyone gave me a hard time, I could flip out like a madman. Startle them into backing off. Luckily, I never had to.

On a better note, it wasn't long before I ran into a friend from my days in Sin City, a dude we called "Yosemite Sam," after his tattoo of the cartoon figure. Doing time for murdering the wife of another friend of ours while high on crack, along with an added sentence for escaping from prison once before, Yosemite Sam and I spent most of our time together. Having him there made the time easier. I no longer felt completely alone.

Mom, Marion, and Billy came to visit once, when I'd been at ACI four months. Mom came to tell me Grandmother Taylor had died. The visit was uncomfortable. I could feel my mother's disappointment, though she tried not to show it. Marion and I barely spoke. I was glad when they didn't return.

After six months, my past bad choices caught up with me again. The call came to report to the warden's office. Right away, I figured the bad checks I'd written or the car I'd stolen from the auto pawn had come to the attention of the Duval County District Attorney. In the warden's office, two US marshals shackled me to a black box for the second time.

One of the marshals looked me squarely in the face. "You've got sixty warrants in your name."

I remained silent, but inside I worried how bad the punishment would be. Was there a way I could talk myself out of this one?

The marshals escorted me in shackles to my dorm cell, allowing me to grab my few personal effects. As I walked through the dorm to my cell, then out, I looked for Yosemite Sam. He was nowhere in sight. Within minutes, I was sitting on another transport van headed back to Jacksonville.

THE YOUNG JITS IN THE DUVAL COUNTY JAIL CROWDED OUT the two men as they grabbed at their meal trays, hoping to hang on to their dinners before the drug-users snatched them away. Tweaking without their dope, the jits moved spastically around the cell, like dancers of a crazy jitterbug. In fact, this crazy dance was how the druggies had earned their nickname. Dressed in my prison clothes, I encountered no resistance or intimidation from the jits. I'd served hard time, unlike the unfortunate young men hoping for a bit of food. I was not to be messed with. The jits stepped out of my way as I walked with my tray across the holding cell.

I'd met with my court-appointed defense attorney two weeks after my transfer to county jail. She'd reassured me that I'd nothing to worry about on the check-fraud charges I'd plead guilty to. Instead of taking ninety days in jail, she'd persuaded me to accept a sentence of a year and a day, a conterminous sentence with my previous time for the strong-arm robbery charge. Considering prior time served, gain time, plus overcrowding, I figured I was close to the end of my sentence. I'd turned twenty-nine waiting in the jail cell with the young jits. If my account and the public defender's advice squared, I'd be released in a matter of weeks, by my end-of-sentence date for the robbery charge.

The day of my EOS, I cleaned up, called my family, and waited for a guard to escort me for release. When no one came by that afternoon, I called for a guard. He had no release paperwork on me. The next day, I tried it again, calling for a guard after no one came for my release. Eventually, a guard came for me.

Instead of being released, the guard put me back on the bus for Lake Butler.

I panicked, shouting out to anyone who'd listen that there'd been a mistake. I was supposed to be going home. My court-appointed lawyer had fouled up. There'd been a terrible misunderstanding. I begged the guards to check into the matter. I couldn't be going back to prison.

I couldn't.

THIS TIME AT LAKE BUTLER THERE WAS NO TALK OF MAKING me a permanent. Though, like before, a guard assigned me to cellblock. I knew better than to claim a medical emergency. This time I faked an ankle injury, on the field in front of a guard. Permanents loaded me onto a stretcher and carried me across the field to the infirmary.

My ankle was still sore, off and on, from my fall at the Gateway treatment center. I figured I'd use the past injury to my advantage. If I suffered an injury and was placed on crutches, they couldn't assign me to the tiered cells of cellblock again. How could I make it up the metal stairs?

One at a time, it turned out.

The guards showed no sympathy for me as I struggled up the cellblock stairs with the crutches for my fake ankle sprain. After ten days, C.O.s came in the night, shackling me for transport, this time to Jefferson Correctional Institute. I left the crutches on the floor next to the bed.

Anger seethed in me. Anger at the system. Anger at my life situation. Anger at myself. I never stopped fighting to convince the warden that the sentence for check fraud was a stupid attorney mistake. I wasn't willing to accept that I deserved everything I got.

I ended up doing four more miserable months.

Upon my release—a hundred bucks in my pocket—I got off the Greyhound bus and walked from downtown toward Grandma White's apartment.

Along Arlington Road, less than three miles from my grandmother's place, an old buddy, Skip, stopped to give me a ride. Instead of going to my family, I drank the beer Skip offered and took a hit off the joint he had in the car. I didn't stop to play through the tape of what I'd do once I took a drink, once I took that first step toward using. I rationalized that I could have just one beer. I could share a joint with my party mate. I could enjoy my freedom again. All my time in prison, the countless dark moments I'd promised myself I was done for good, was no defense. I was defenseless.

I was powerless.

I was back.

I was high on crack by nightfall.

Skip dropped me off in a dope hole in Sin City, not far from Grandma's house. Police officers stopped me coming out of the area, after I'd gotten high. I didn't have drugs on me, but I knew they knew the deal. I told them I'd just gotten out of prison that morning, headed to my grandmother's house. The officers ran my name. Since my last arrest, the DA's office had filed more check-fraud charges. The outstanding warrants waited for me, like traps of my own setting. I'd stepped off the Greyhound bus and right into one.

This time I wasn't angry. I was scared. As the cops drove me back downtown to the jailhouse that seemed like my second home, I knew for sure—surer than I'd ever known—that I was sick. Really sick. I was an addict, and there was no stopping me from using, no fighting it.

I might as well give in.

So our troubles, we think, are basically
of our own making.

A.A. WORLD SERVICE, INC.,
ALCOHOLICS ANONYMOUS, "HOW IT WORKS"

Chapter 18

A Powerful Disease

As I SAT IN JAIL ON THE NEW WARRANTS, THE awareness that I was powerless over my addiction weighed upon me. The insanity of it had been that my mind wouldn't let me stay in that acceptance mode for very long. I could tell myself—as I'd done a thousand times—that I could stop, that I *would* stop. I told myself I had the power and the will to quit using cocaine.

As I stared at the jail cell walls, a moment of clarity washed over me. I couldn't stop. I could no more stop using than I could stop being myself. This was who I was: Timothy White—my father's only son; the guy who'd lied, cheated, and scammed to get high; a drug addict.

Over the next six months, police repeatedly arrested me on check-fraud charges—seven or so times, three or four checks at a time. Overall, the DA filed eighty-eight separate counts of writing worthless checks. I'd serve a period in county jail and be released, only to be picked up again.

After a while, I no longer cared. I took up with an ex-stepbrother, a guy whose mother had married and divorced my father. I remembered Dot, Brad's mother, fondly, though her and my father's marriage hadn't lasted long. Though we got along, living with Brad brought back those chaotic times in Sin City as a child with my father, only helping to keep me in my own chaotic state of mind.

Brad let me move in with him and his girlfriend. Our days were a nonstop maelstrom of drinking, drug use, and insanity. I worked roofing but nothing steady. I knew all the dope holes in Jacksonville, and Brad and his girlfriend often relied on me to score for them.

One night, Brad gave me sixty dollars to buy us crack. I'd gone to a familiar spot, but my usual connection hadn't been around. I scored from a guy I didn't know. By the time I realized the guy had scammed me, it was too late. I knew I couldn't go back with fake rock and no money.

I hid out after that episode. On Friday evening, I took a portion of the money I'd earned the last few days roofing houses and bought a pair of loafers from Kinney Shoes. I spent thirty dollars, which to me was a decent amount of money for a pair of shoes, but I'd needed a new pair. The rest of the money I spent on food, cigarettes, beer, gas for the car, and, of course, crack. I couldn't go back to Brad's, so I drove between friends' houses and dope holes, drinking and getting high until I ran out of cash. I didn't want to pull more scams and couldn't fall back on a box of blank checks. I did the only thing I could think of.

The Kinney's shoebox still lay with the receipt in the back of my car. I'd worn the shoes the last few days, my old pair trashed as soon as I bought new ones. Barefoot, I walked into Kinney's to return the shoes. To me, they still looked returnable. So what if I'd worn them a few days? The sales person put up no fuss, and I headed straight for a crack dealer. I needed to get high. The only thing that meant anything to me at that moment was hitting the pipe. If I could have, I would have stayed high—a constant, glorious, oblivious high.

Thirty dollars plus tax didn't last long. After several days of staying high and with no sleep, I crashed in my car, which had run out of gas downtown, coasting on fumes into a parking lot off Jessie Street, about a mile away from the detox center. I knew I'd nowhere to go. Going back to Brad's meant facing them without their money or dope and likely getting the tar beat out of me. I'd burnt just about every bridge by then—Mom, Grandma White, Mitch, even my brother Billy.

I was a wretch, a small, bug-like creature. Sick, shoeless, and consumed with my own sense of worthlessness, I walked over gravel and bits of broken glass the mile to the detox center. I could think of no other choice.

They had to take me in, right? I mean, I'd been there before. They'd made a place for me until a treatment bed had opened at Gateway. I'd failed at treatment, but I figured they had to take me in again—at least for now.

Like the six-year-old boy I'd been in Grandma White's backyard twenty-three years earlier, I entered the detox unit barefoot, seeking help, not from God this time but from medical staff that might help me find a cure for this awful madness. I'll never forget how low and small I felt—or the look on the intake nurse's face.

The middle-age woman with supple-looking black skin and dressed in bright blue scrubs looked me up and down. "Boy, you sure are handsome! You ought to be on TV."

I couldn't believe this woman. I felt like a roach. A vile creature. I couldn't imagine how I looked. I was trying hard just to not throw up on my bare feet. A dark and deep depression washed over me, drowned me in its oppressive weight. A staff member took me to the clothes closet for a pair of shoes, two sizes too small. I squeezed my feet into them anyway and spent a week in the too-small shoes, feet blistered and soul broken.

Reluctantly, I agreed to return to Gateway Services for a second time. After a week, I contacted Brad, coming up with some story about being stopped by the cops, almost OD'ing, making excuses that covered the period from when I'd left his house for crack and ended up calling him. Brad bought the lie. I was always convincing, ever the manipulator. He and his girlfriend visited, bringing me a pair of tennis shoes and a pack of cigarettes. I was thankful for his kindness, but, of course, I stuck with my fake story about the cop or whatever I'd come up with to cover my tracks.

Gateway allowed me to rest and recover for a few weeks. I had no intention, though, of making it through drug and alcohol treatment. I'd tried it. It didn't take. I was in treatment the second time for a few weeks. The night before I left the center, I argued with a staff member, a counselor who tried to make me see the path I was headed down.

The woman stood close to me, inches from my face, and said loudly, "Well, you might just have to be one of the people who have to die."

"Well, I *might* just be!" I yelled back.

I wasn't in the mindset for recovery. Brad wasn't mad at me anymore. I'd snowed him. I felt rested and ready to go back out.

I left the next morning, back to the chaos. Back to the life that led me again and again to the same places.

I smoked crack the first night out of Gateway. A drug dealer came to Brad's house with rock. Brad tried to be good about it. I remember how he looked at me, the concern obvious in his expression, and said, "Man, are you all right with this? I mean, like you're okay, right?"

"Yeah, yeah, man," I reassured him. "I'm fine now."

I was off and running that night. No sense wasting a perfectly good opportunity to get high. I couldn't blame Brad or his girlfriend. They had no idea that I couldn't watch them smoke crack and not use myself.

I didn't stay with Brad much longer. I'd worn out my welcome. Besides, I'd come up with a plan to put some distance between Jacksonville and me.

First, I tried going back to Keystone Heights, to stay with my mother and Billy. Being so close to Starke and the drug spots and dealers I knew there proved too tempting. I ran with some of the old crowd and some new folks, including a hot blonde who joined me in a two-week joy ride in a car we stole from an older gentleman friend of hers.

We borrowed the man's car, supposedly to go to the store, drove fifty miles to Lake City, Florida, to pick up a friend of mine, then went on a rip and roar all over the state, scamming and hustling. We boosted merchandise from stores, then returned the items for cash. We pulled scams at grocery stores, shoving meat down our pants and stealing cartons of cigarettes. We stole fishing equipment, expensive rods and reels, then broke them and returned to complain about the broken merchandise we'd found upon opening the box, demanding our money back.

It took me no time to become a pro at the criminal activity. So good at lying straight-faced to a clerk or manager, I reveled in what I could pull off. I could get over on anyone. The adrenaline rush from boosting and hustling pumped me up, kept me charging full-speed ahead. I liked the way I could con others and get what I wanted.

I spoke with an accent, going into a store as one person, then returning minutes later in different clothes and with a different voice and mannerisms to get cash for the item I'd just stolen. In short time, I became addicted to the rush of my criminal activity.

At one point, I hooked up with a guy who'd recently gone AWOL from the navy. With a navy ID, he could shoplift items from the exchange and bring them right back in for a return.

The run came to an abrupt halt back in Jacksonville, in an Albertson's Grocery parking lot. I ran out of the store's automatic double doors with a package of steaks shoved down my pants, the navy guy waiting for me in a stolen jeep. As I made it to the front door, one of only a few customers in the middle of the night, the manager stepped in front of me, directing me to stop. I pushed him aside. As I ran out the door, a Jacksonville police officer, who happened to be entering, grabbed hold of me and shoved me to the ground. The officer scraped my face across the parking lot surface as he pulled my arms back and cuffed me.

"Do you quit? Do you quit?" the cop yelled.

When he'd pushed me to the ground, he'd broken my foot. An ambulance rushed me to the hospital. I never saw or heard from the navy guy again.

I served a month in jail for shoplifting. While I did my time, the craziness of it all hit me. I'd left Jacksonville, tried to leave the drug scene. Instead of making better choices, I'd started stealing and running scams. I'd learned nothing. I told myself—again—that I could do better. I could change.

My foot broken, and worn out from running hard for several months, I called Billy for a ride back to Keystone Heights and my mother's house. I left jail on crutches, determined to quit using and make something better for myself. I'd start over fresh, in a place that had lots of work for me and my brother Billy, who'd agreed to help me get back on my feet. I'd go somewhere that promised to be better. Recent tropical storm damage had left parts of Florida with roofs that needed repair. Work would keep me straight. Plenty of it waited for me further south.

Billy and I left for Daytona Beach eager to work.

Anticipating a change and brighter days, I told myself that I could keep it together. I could get along like normal folks. My past didn't have to be my future. Life could be different. I just needed to get away from the people and places I knew before. I could gain control. Better days lay ahead.

I told myself many things.

It is a curious sensation: the sort of pain that goes mercifully beyond our powers of feeling. When your heart is broken, your boats are burned: nothing matters any more. It is the end of happiness and the beginning of peace.

GEORGE BERNARD SHAW

CHAPTER 19

Daytona Days and Durham Nights

THE CHEAP EFFICIENCY HOTEL SAT ON A1A, ALONG the opposite side of the ocean on the Daytona Beach strip, a hole in the wall but good enough for Billy and me. All I needed was an honest way to make money and the strength to keep my head on straight. Make smart decisions. Being around my brother felt good. We got along. He'd never been the kind of partier that I'd been. He could handle drinking and not go overboard.

At first, Daytona seemed like the perfect solution, or at least if not perfect, than manageable. We found work roofing right away. The early summer heat beating down on me as I ripped damaged roof shingles away reminded me what it felt like to do good, hard work. When the temperature cooled at night, though, I hated being stuck in the small hotel room. I knew no one but Billy and the guys I worked with, but my outgoing personality made it easy for me to make friends. I began to feel a familiar unease and restlessness. It wasn't long before I found interesting distractions, a way to spend my evenings: namely in the form of Mattie Kowalski.

A fleabag motel sat a block away, a full-blown drug den. Everyone there, including the motel manager, either smoked crack or sold crack or both. It seemed you couldn't rent a room there if you weren't using or selling. Mattie stayed at the motel. A few years younger than me at twenty-six, she survived turning tricks and hooking up with guys like me who were attracted to her bleach-blonde hair, sky-blue eyes, and wild nature. Mattie loved a good time and crack rock. She was exactly the kind of girl I needed to stay far, far from. Of course, I couldn't stay away.

Within a week of meeting her, I ditched the roofing job. I couldn't stay up with Mattie smoking crack all night and shingle roofs under the sizzling sun all day. Yeah, I'd gone to Daytona to get my head on straight and get away from the bad decisions I'd made before, but loyalty to Billy and holding down a job proved no match against the pull of Mattie and the excitement she offered. Soon, Billy left for Keystone Heights, making it clear he did not intend to watch me do myself in again.

That was fine by me.

I'd still need money, though, to pay for a hotel room, to eat, but mostly to buy crack. We stayed as high as we could, as long as we could. I didn't need to work. Mattie had her body to earn money, and I became her pimp. Before smoking crack—back in the days when Julie and I lived at Uncle David's house, back when it felt I still had a conscience and a soul—the idea of being a woman's pimp would have disgusted me. Certainly, I was no saint and familiar to the business of prostitution, but I'd never been this close to it, let alone a full player in transactions. My desire for crack drowned out my conscience and any objections I had. I entered into her world willingly, not even blinking at how quickly I adapted to the lifestyle.

Mattie could sell her body and make us money. Or—and this was faster and more profitable—she could lure a man into a promise of sexual services, then I would barge into the room, beat the living crap out of the guy, and take whatever money he had. Rolling johns seemed preferable to having my girlfriend perform sex acts for our needs.

Another way we made money—mostly me and not Mattie—was to "beat" the tourists, scamming them with fake drugs or the promise of a drug score. The place to party, Daytona teemed with tourists ready to buy marijuana, pills, acid, cocaine . . . whatever. I'd walk the beach with bottles of aspirin or lidocaine powder that I could pass off as pills or cocaine. We'd befriend tourists on the beach or the strip, strike up a conversation, then con them into buying whatever we'd manufactured or hand us money with the understanding that we'd return shortly with what they needed.

The tourist beats were lowlife rip-offs, immature stuff, but assaulting johns for whatever they had in their pockets was serious, dangerous, and on one occasion, nearly fatal.

Most of the men were older, businessmen in town for work. Sometimes Mattie and I would pair up with another girl and guy working the strip. We'd go from one hotel to the next. One or both of the girls would pick a guy up in a hotel bar, then take him back to his room. We stuck to the hotels and motels with outside accommodations. A flashing outdoor light meant the guy had removed his clothes. By myself, or with the other girl's boyfriend, I would bomb-rush the room, scaring the john as he lay naked and defenseless in bed. I'd scream about how Mattie was my girlfriend and he was messing with my woman. I'd kick over chairs and threaten to bash the guy's head in. While we'd terrify the man, the girls would clean out his pockets. Sometimes, especially if the john looked as if he might put up any resistance, we'd knock the guy out. One time, in particular, events turned even more dangerous.

From the start, the big-mouthed Yankee grated my nerves.

We'd planned to roll someone that night. Mattie and I were with another couple, and the girls focused on the young guy from up north who claimed to be a boxer, bragging to everyone in the hotel bar about his prizefighting skills. While the other businessmen cowered when we rushed the room, this guy bowed up. Half-undressed, propped up against the hotel bed's headboard, he cursed us, shouting vile slurs at the girls.

Ignoring the fact that we were there to rob him, I wasn't going to let this punk talk to Mattie that way. Hyped up on drugs and determined, in some twisted way, to defend Mattie's honor, I rushed to retrieve a knife I'd left in the couple's car. When I returned with my blade, the girl's boyfriend had punched the Yankee so hard the punk's jawbone stuck out. The man clutched at his face. Blood flowed down his neck as he tried desperately to shield himself from further blows.

The man's faded blue jeans lay crumpled at the foot of the bed. I reached into the front pocket and retrieved a large roll of bills, over $1,800 we'd count later. After I stuffed the money into my pocket, I sprung the switchblade and held it to the guy's throat. Anger flashed through me. My heart thumped in my chest. This guy had intended to have sex with Mattie, then called her nasty names.

I pictured myself slicing his throat. Almost gleefully, I imagined what it might look like, blood spurting in all directions as I drew the sharp blade across his thick neck. It would feel good to work my anger out on this worthless piece of garbage.

Thankfully a moment of reason came over me, and I pulled back the blade. I could see myself doing it, could picture it so clearly, but I couldn't follow through. I'd only wanted to scare the guy. From the terror in his eyes, he'd been scared for his life all right. Besides, the girl's boyfriend had already done severe damage to his face. He was never going to forget us.

The john's money burning in my pocket, we got out of there fast.

AS CRAZY AS IT SOUNDS, I FELL IN LOVE WITH MATTIE. WITH her, I could be as addicted to substances and insane acting as I wanted, without judgment. I'd no sense to realize that her lack of condemnation was because she was lost in her own addiction. I thought she loved me, too. We were up against the world together. We tore through Daytona like wild animals, caged for our entire lives and now set free to do whatever to whomever we wished.

It wasn't long, though, before there wasn't a hotel in town that hadn't banned us. We talked people into renting hotel rooms for us, just so we'd have a bed to sleep in. Cops arrested me four times for shoplifting, and I was sure my picture or description was behind every customer service counter in town. We couldn't move around the beach without the chance of running into someone we'd conned, or worse. I grew a beard and slunk around, paranoid that I'd run into someone I'd robbed or beaten up. Awake for days at a time, sometimes as long as five days straight, I hallucinated and, at one point, found myself having fallen asleep walking down A1A in the middle of traffic.

The people we associated with were as criminal and chaotic as we were. For a while, we came out only after dark, scurrying like cockroaches at any cast of light. We were the dregs of society, living in a cesspool. I felt the wretchedness cover me like thick tar. The time had come to leave. Daytona had played out for us—and us for it.

MATTIE HAD PEOPLE IN DURHAM, NORTH CAROLINA— people we could stay with and a way to keep using. With the money she'd swiped from a john, a young, drunk guy who had his payroll in his pocket, we bought a clunker of a car, slapped on a stolen tag, and headed north. The November air chilled us as we drove from Daytona to Durham, stopping along the way to scam money from convenience stores. After buying the car, a tank of gas, and dope, we soon ran out of funds. By fifty miles out of Daytona, we were flat broke. Worse, Mattie was sick the whole way. Whether she was sick from lack of proper nutrition, some reaction to drugs, or a case of flu, Mattie lay curled in a ball on the passenger-side most of the way to Durham.

My scams brought in money for gas and the little bit of food we ate along the way. I'd become so good at hustling store clerks and so bold that I no longer even left the store, picking up a ten-dollar bottle of medication from the shelf and walking right up to the cashier to complain that my wife had bought the wrong type. I was allergic and needed my money back to buy the right kind somewhere else. We made it to Durham ten bucks at a time.

Mattie had been a drug addict in Durham with a long criminal record, so it was no surprise to her that our first night in town, cops pulled us over on suspicion of questionable activity. Arriving into town, we'd gone straight to an apartment complex where Mattie knew drug dealers where we could score. We got high at the dealer's apartment, smoking all the rock we had money to buy. Police officers pulled us over coming out of the complex. They knew Mattie on sight.

A large cop shined his flashlight in our eyes and whistled softly. He looked past me in the driver's seat, nodding his head at Mattie. "Damn girl, where you been?"

The officer arrested her immediately for outstanding warrants. I gave him my brother Billy's name. After he handcuffed Mattie, he looked at me. "Unless you want to go to jail, start walking."

"Start walking?" I repeated. "Can I get my coat?"

The cop's voice lowered. "No, you can't get anything. Start walking."

I did as the cop said, leaving the car and my coat behind. I was cold, alone, and clueless as to my exact whereabouts. That first night, I walked to an abandoned area and found cardboard boxes to cover myself against the cold and wind.

The next morning, I walked downtown to a Salvation Army. I'd no money and bummed change outside of a Wendy's to buy a cup of coffee. I'd bummed plenty of change over the years, but now—without a coat and alone in a city I didn't know—I felt like a bum, destitute. Before, as a child, I'd entertained the men in the bar on 8th Street for their loose coins. As a teenager, I'd bummed dimes for sodas and snack cakes. None of those times made me feel like this. In a few months, I'd transformed into a bum, a homeless vagrant.

In the line at the Salvation Army, another homeless man handed me a coat. He wore one coat on him. His extra coat, he gave to me. His kindness, this unknown stranger, touches me still today. I put on the coat and waited in line for my first meal in Durham: a pack of peanuts and a banana.

The Salvation Army allowed me to stay a few days. At a nearby business, I could get an ID without proof of identification. I gave the guy behind the counter Billy's name and birth date. I was too afraid to give my real name. The fake ID would let me into the jail to see Mattie. During the drive from Florida, she'd told me of an old couple she knew in Raleigh who had money. The talk was that I'd contact a guy she knew, and he'd give me a ride to Raleigh to rob the couple. At the jail, Mattie gave me the phone number of the guy and assured me that the couple had money and would be easy targets. With the money I could get from the robbery, I could bail her out of jail. Then, we'd be back together again.

The guy she knew was a real oddball. Short, heavyset, and with a long face, he looked like a fat rodent of some type. Perhaps in my condition—with my unkempt beard, dirty clothes, and nervous energy—I was the odd-looking and strange-acting one. I hadn't slept well for days. I remember getting into the guy's van and thinking that he seemed hesitant to be around me. He said he'd drive me to the couple's house but that was all. I was on my own from there.

We drove past the house as he promised, but then he took a detour and headed back downtown. I tried talking to the guy, trying to talk him into taking me back to the old couple's house or at least their neighborhood.

Instead, he stopped his van in the middle of traffic and jumped out, running to a nearby cop who was getting out of his squad car. He yelled to the cop that he wanted me out of his van. He didn't say that I was planning a crime but went off about how he didn't want to be near me. I jumped out of the van, in downtown Raleigh, without a way back to Durham and Mattie. I knew she wanted out of jail and needed me, so I found my way back to the targeted location with the mindset that I'd do the job.

I hung out near the couple's house, in the bushes. After it got dark, I fell asleep. I woke up in the middle of the night. I could see the lights were out in the house, but I couldn't bring myself to take action. I played it over in my mind. I'd break in through the back door; tie up the couple with whatever I could find; take whatever cash they had, maybe fine jewelry or watches. The more I tried to convince myself I could do it, the more I talked myself out of it. In the end, I couldn't go through with it. I was sure I'd get caught.

I thumbed back to Durham, empty-handed.

I spent the next few nights in a homeless shelter. I'd hang around the shelter most of the day, aiming to be first in line to get a bed at night. Sometimes, I tried swindling stores, shoplifting items to return for cash. Looking as I did, clerks kept a closer eye on me than they had in Daytona.

The shelter was a roof over my head, but the conditions depressed me. I felt demoralized. I remember trying to sleep on a tiny cot one evening when an old man stood beside me, swaying slightly, staring blankly at me. I watched in amazement and disgust as he urinated on himself, the patch of wetness spreading across the front of his dirty pants then flowing out across the linoleum floor. I had to see Mattie and find somewhere else to stay.

I don't remember what I told Mattie about my failure to execute her robbery plan. She tried hooking me up with her friends, other drug-users she'd partied with in the past. None of them seemed to want me around for long. One couple let me sleep on their porch for a week or so. Young and unemployed, they lived with the guy's mother. Like me, they smoked crack, but, unlike me, they had a bit of stability and good sense, enough sense to keep me on the porch at night, along with their German shepherd. All night long, the dog and I fought over who got to sleep on the porch's beat-up couch. I'd sunk to a point so low that I fought a dog for his bed. I couldn't wait for Mattie to be released.

At night, I broke into cars and, a few times, into churches, stealing whatever I could get my hands on that I could sell easily. I was running out of porches to sleep on. I needed a decent place to crash—*and money to use*. I couldn't go on this way and did what came naturally. I called a roofing company and found some daywork. With the little money I earned, I rented a room in a boarding house. Mattie was to be released in a month. I figured that I would find even better work as soon as I could. Then, she and I could move into a nice place together.

The neighborhood around the boarding house thronged with folks in my condition, many addicted to alcohol and drugs, dysfunctional and often living in denial about their illness. I met a young girl who worked as an escort. For a few weeks, we hung together. Ours was merely a platonic friendship, more based on my ability to score drugs for her and my loneliness than anything else. She worked with a much higher class of clientele than did Mattie. A few times, she drove me to affluent neighborhoods where I broke into houses, taking small items and whatever cash I could find.

On one particular night, when we'd run out of money for drugs, I had her take me to a nice neighborhood. Nothing stirred on the streets at 2:00 A.M. except for us, desperate for a high. We drove the ritzy neighborhood with its two-story homes and manicured lawns. After a trip around a few square blocks, we settled on a house, pulling up in front of the garage.

I leaned over toward her as she sat in the driver's seat. "Pick me back up here in fifteen minutes." I took off my shoes, throwing them on the back seat. I didn't want to make noise walking through the house, and I couldn't carry my sneakers with me.

I got out of the car barefooted and headed toward the garage. With a wave from me, the girl took off. I watched as she drove down the street and around a corner. The noise of her car engine faded, and, once again, the street went quiet. I walked slowly up to the garage, breaking my way inside. Rooting around in the pitch black for something to steal, I tried my best not to make a sound.

Before I could find anything of value, a deep voice trumpeted in the darkness. "What are you doing in here?"

I bolted from the garage and into the backyard, the voice following behind me, yelling and swearing. Over my shoulder, I screamed, "I've got a gun!" Maybe that would stop his pursuit.

I jumped the back fence, flaying my upper arm open. Blood rushed down my arm. As I ran, I wiped the blood across my short-sleeved shirt. The mid-December night air stung my face. My blood-soaked shirt clung to my chest, getter colder by the minute as I looked up and down the street for the girl's car. Anger rushed through my body. I was sure at any moment that the neighborhood would be swarming with cops.

I walked toward a patch of lights down the road, which turned out to be a school. Prying open the doors of a school bus parked to the side of the bus-loading loop, I lay down in a defeated, exhausted heap. My arm had stopped bleeding. Either the cut had not been as bad as I thought, or the cold had help stop the bleeding. My brain felt numb, and I could think of nothing to help my situation. I shivered until I fell asleep.

I awoke to the sounds of children laughing and yelling. From the high-pitch sound of the voices, the school had to be for elementary students. Luckily, no bus driver had needed the bus that morning. I opened the school bus doors and walked away. No one stopped me. Strangely, no one even seemed to notice me.

Waves of anger and desperation crashed over me again. My uncovered feet ached, and my arm hurt where I'd cut it open. The cold air whipped through my flimsy shirt. The blood had dried, but the thin cotton material was no match against the December morning chill. The smell of my own sweat and blood, and the undercurrent of some foul odor that likely came from the school bus, nauseated me. I wanted to get high so badly that I would do anything.

A half-mile or so from the school, I cut across a lawn, toward a house with no cars in the driveway. Always a good sign. I broke the window of the back door and made my way inside. The place looked tidy and smelled clean. Sunlight streamed from the windows into a brightly painted kitchen. A small, yappy dog, maybe a Yorkie, barked at me. I paid the dog no mind. In my mood, he should have been happy that I didn't kick him across the room.

A small, metal cashbox sat on the kitchen table, almost as if it were a present, waiting for my arrival. Inside the box were one-dollar bills and loose coins. I shoved the bills and change into my jeans' front pocket. At the bottom of the box lay a checkbook. I opened the checkbook and ripped out a check. I folded the check and slid it into my back pocket.

I wasted no time getting out of the house. I'd no idea where I was or how to get back to the boarding house. With the bills in my front pocket, I found a pay phone and called for a cab. Back at the boarding house, I counted out the money, relieved to see a few tens and fives as well as the singles. Even after the cab ride, I netted over sixty dollars. My mood picked up a bit. Then, I remembered the check in my back pocket. I could forge the check, bringing in more money, maybe enough to have some left when Mattie got out the next week.

I pulled the check from my back pocket and unfolded it. It took a moment for me to process what I read at the upper-left corner of the check. *Alcoholics Anonymous*, it read. I dropped the check to the floor like it was a hot poker. It couldn't be possible. Of all the houses to rob, I'd managed to find the home of a treasurer for an AA group. I flashed to the Twelve-Step meetings I'd attended through Gateway and after, during my short period of recovery. Was this a sign from God? Could it just be chance? My transgression had led me to cross paths again with a Twelve-Step program. The check sat on the stained carpet until I collected my thoughts. Then, it sat in the wastebasket, in a dozen little pieces.

AFTER THE AA EPISODE, I CONTINUED TO BURGLARIZE homes and cars, along with a few businesses. My questions about signs from God were overridden by my need for drugs, and I quickly pushed away any hesitation or guilt. Mattie's release meant that I had a partner again. I knew she wouldn't drive off and leave me stranded in an unknown area of town in the middle of the night. The fact that her arrest had done basically that—left me stranded and alone—evaded me. I thought I could trust her. Right away, she went back to prostitution to support her—and my—habit. I swallowed my pride and came to terms that she'd need to sell herself for drugs and money.

Actually, Mattie's release kept me sane. When she got out, she reconnected with her people. None of them cared for me, though. Drinking all the time and high whenever possible, I was no joy to be around. Her friends complained that I was loud and aggressive. One woman swore that I'd pushed her kid while getting high at the woman's house. I have no recollection of having pushed any kid, but I know that I was losing grip with reality, lost in a constant haze of booze and crack.

Around that time, I called my mother and asked her to send me money for a bus ticket home. Before Mattie's release, I'd thought about going back to Keystone Heights, shaking off Durham and all the mess I'd found myself in. More than likely, though, I wanted the money for crack. I'd stopped the daywork. I was blowing through cash like feeding peanuts to circus elephants: at some point, you end up tossing the whole bag their way. Mattie worked the street. I stole whatever I could find easily and sell quickly and served a short stint in the Durham city jail for shoplifting.

Mom came through, though, sending me a nonrefundable, one-way ticket to Starke. I couldn't cash the ticket in, so I stuffed it into a duffle bag and promptly put it out of my mind.

The morning the cops came for Mattie, we'd stayed up half the night and slept in late. I heard a loud thump against the side of the house, next to the window by our bed. Mattie lay curled up next to me. Her hair smelled of cheap perfume and cigarette smoke.

From over her shoulder, as if in slow motion, I watched a cop climb a ladder. Through my foggy mental haze, I realized the ladder had been the thump I'd heard. Our room was on the second floor. I guess the police had knocked on the house front door and got no answer. Apparently, they meant to make their way inside.

The sound of fists pounding against the room's door caused me to spring from the bed, now fully alert. I knew if I didn't open the door, the cop at the window planned on coming through, one way or the other.

I let the cops at the door into the room. Apparently, Mattie had violated her bail. They were there to take her back to jail. I knew it was the end of the line for her—and for us. I'd become a one-man crime wave in Durham. If she talked at all, they'd be right back for me. I didn't know if she would give me up for anything. Perhaps if they held serious jail time over her head, pumped her for information that might help them close any open cases. I couldn't be sure, and I couldn't handle more time alone in Durham without her.

After the cops took her away—with barely time for me to say good-bye—I grabbed what little I had, stuffed it into the duffle bag, and walked down to the bus station. Thank God for my mother sending the ticket.

By noon, I was on my way back to Florida.

Acceptance of one's life has nothing
to do with resignation; it does not
mean running away from the struggle.
On the contrary, it means accepting it
as it comes, with all the handicaps
of heredity, of suffering, of psychological
complexes and injustices.
PAUL TOURNIER

CHAPTER 20
Crossroads

MY MOTHER'S TEARS BEGAN THE MOMENT I STEPPED off the bus from Durham. She and Billy had come to meet me at the Greyhound bus stop in Starke. Seven months had passed since I'd last seen my mother. New Year's Eve of 1993 was just days away. When last I'd gotten a good look at myself, in the bathroom mirror of a gas station between North Carolina and Florida, I noted my physical deterioration. Surrounded by dark purplish circles, my eyes had sunken in. I'd lost at least twenty-five pounds off my already slender frame. My clothes hung loosely on my gaunt figure, and I reeked of cigarettes, beer, and human funk.

Was I even human? I felt less than human—sub-subhuman. Insectile.

I tried to smile at my mother, which only made her cry harder. Billy took my duffle bag and told me everything would be okay. He was glad I was home.

I spent the next few days in a strange mental place, uncomfortable with my surroundings. I was an imposter, like a bad celebrity impersonator. I tried to be normal around my family but found myself having slipped so far from any center point that I came off sounding awkward and skewed. Much of the talk centered on fattening me up and getting me back to work and "on track." I decided the only way to get my life in order was to turn myself in, and that's what I swore to them I would do.

My mother had put up her only possession of value, a camper trailer, to secure my bond. Because I'd jumped bond on the latter warrants for check fraud, the bail bondsman was threatening to repossess her trailer. The only way I could keep that from happening meant walking up to a police station and handing myself over to the authorities. I feared being caught for crimes in Daytona and Durham, but I couldn't let my mother lose her trailer—or continue to disappoint her. I was sick and beaten down.

My mother's kindness and understanding touched a place in my heart that had been dead for years. I needed more than a mother's love, however, to turn myself over to the police. I needed a father's strength. I turned to Mitch for that strength. Billy drove me to Mitch's house in Jacksonville Beach. With him, I marched up to the front counter at the Jacksonville Sherriff's Office on Bay Street and announced to the officer on duty that they had a warrant for my arrest. The officer behind the counter turned out to be a school chum of Mitch's.

The officer checked the records, then looked back at me and said, "I'm not finding anything here."

Without a hiccup, I said, "You're not finding anything?"

"No," the officer insisted, looking at me with a sideways glance, then at Mitch.

I said nothing back to the officer and beat it out the building. I knew there was a warrant, but if they didn't know about it, who was I to insist they lock me up?

Reluctantly, Mitch drove me to Starke. He'd offered to drive me back to Keystone Heights, to my mother's house. I couldn't buy crack in Keystone and wanted to get high in the worst way. I hadn't used since stepping off the Greyhound bus and my addiction screamed at me to be fed. With a BS story about someone I had to talk to or whatever, I convinced Mitch to give me twenty dollars and drop me off in downtown Starke. Then, I raced to the nearest dope hole.

That day would be the last time I smoked crack, in a grimy Texaco gas station off US Highway 301.

All the times I'd told myself I'd stop—*I had to stop*—that day, in that dirty, tiny bathroom, wasn't one of those times. No fanfare sounded. I performed no sacred ritual, said no solemn good-bye to the drug that had entrapped and bound my heart, mind, and soul for the past nine years. In fact, the inferior product produced a miserable high. Looking back, I'm glad it ended that way—in the cramped, filthy stench that the gas station bathroom represented.

It seems fitting.

AFTER SMOKING THE CRACK BOUGHT WITH MITCH'S twenty dollars, I experienced an immediate need for more. I considered my limited cash-generating options and decided to shoplift from a nearby Walmart. I'd boosted merchandise from Daytona to Durham, but now my hands shook—just slightly but enough to throw me off. I'd little confidence in my boosting skills in my condition. Instead of stealing, I called Billy. He'd given me money more times in the past than I could count. I figured he'd reach in his pocket to help me again.

I called my brother from a payphone on the corner of State Road 100 and Southeast County Road 100A, near the CSX railroad tracks and the bar I'd torn half my hide off breaking into five years earlier. Five years had worn me down. Crack and alcohol had stripped me of my pride, my relationships, my work, my dignity. I sat on the curb where, nearby, I'd run out on a restaurant check as a teenager, hitched rides into dope holes to feed my addiction, stolen newspapers to cover myself as I slept in the woods on a winter night, and severely injured myself for stolen cash to buy drugs. I was broken and devoid of hope, but I sat waiting for Billy to give me a few more dollars to use.

How could I recover from this place? How could I find strength and hope? Nothing had stopped me. My willpower had not been enough. My family, friends, and lovers had not been enough. Detox and treatment, even prison, had not been enough. I would be forever an addict. My father had been, and I would be, too. Was I even worthy of any better life than this? I wrapped my arms around myself, against the cold of the January night air, and thought of how I'd ended up on this curb.

What did it matter in the end? At this point, no one or nothing could help me. I was too far gone.

Turns out, Billy had reached his end as well. He wouldn't give me a dime. Not even for a beer to calm my nerves. I could understand saying no to money for crack, but I'd drank since I was a kid. We both had. I thank him now; it was the right thing to do. At the time, though, anger welled in me, but I felt too sick and depressed to express it. Billy reached out his hand and helped me off the curb. I rode back to Billy's house slumped in the backseat of his car.

Billy was living out in the countryside with a woman named Roseanne. I still knew I needed to turn myself in. I'd done so much wrong, committed so many crimes, that I stayed on high alert, worried the cops would show up to arrest me on new charges. I was willing to go back to jail on the outstanding warrants. If I didn't, my mother would lose her camper. Confessing to new crimes, though, wasn't in my plans.

The next several days passed like a bizarre dream.

I didn't use. Though I'd no real hope of getting and staying clean, my body couldn't take more abuse. Partly from withdrawal, partly from exhaustion, my head ached and my stomach stayed tied in knots. I'd never felt so fatigued. Utterly depleted.

When I wasn't sleeping, I walked the country roads outside Billy's house, his Walkman radio streaming music into my brain. The music mixed with strange thoughts and images of my family and friends that floated before my eyes. In their faces, I saw how I'd wounded them, felt how done they were with me. I was near the end. Images of my father and Grandma White, of my mother and brothers, of Julie and Raymond and Mitch, and even Mattie—*everyone I'd taken for granted, used, and disappointed*—floated before me. I told them how sorry I was, how ashamed. I promised to fix it all. Going back to the police and insisting they find the warrant would fix everything, and if not *everything*, then enough to keep me sane for now.

If I could not set things a little right, I feared I might lose my mind.

The period at Billy's lasted less than a week. I had to get back to Jacksonville and do it right this time. Billy drove me back to Mitch's house, and Mitch and I made plans to go back to the Jacksonville

Sheriff's Office the next afternoon. As events played out, JSO and the bail bondsman beat us to the punch.

I stood in the kitchen of Mitch's home in Jacksonville Beach making a ham and cheese sandwich. After lunch, we planned to drive downtown to turn myself over. A noise from outside caught my attention, and I laid the butter knife on the kitchen counter. Seconds later, two policemen and the bondsman stormed the kitchen. So detached from reality and resigned to my fate, I asked the officers if I could take my sandwich with me to eat on the way. Remarkably, they agreed.

To this day, I'm unsure how the bondsman knew I was there. I've a faint recollection that maybe I called him at one point between going to Mitch's house the first time to turn myself in and returning the second time after failing my first attempt. Mitch had known the officer on duty at the Sherriff's office that day. Maybe JSO had found the arrest warrant and connected me with Mitch. I'm still unclear on that point. Maybe a neighbor or—and I highly doubt this but anything is possible—Mitch or Billy called the bondsman and told him where I could be found. Regardless, the bondsman brought me in and the deed was done at last.

I'm grateful for whatever way it happened.

THE 12 STEPS OF NARCOTICS ANONYMOUS

1. We admitted we were powerless over our addiction, that our lives had become unmanageable.

2. We came to believe that a Power greater than ourselves could restore us to sanity.

3. We made a decision to turn our will and our lives over to the care of God *as we understood Him.*

4. We made a searching and fearless moral inventory of ourselves.

5. We admitted to God, to ourselves, and to another human being the exact nature of our wrongs.

6. We were entirely ready to have God remove all these defects of character.

7. We humbly asked Him to remove our shortcomings.

8. We made a list of all persons we had harmed, and became willing to make amends to them all.

9. We made direct amends to such people wherever possible, except when to do so would injure them or others.

10. We continued to take personal inventory and when we were wrong promptly admitted it.

11. We sought through prayer and meditation to improve our conscious contact with God *as we understood Him, praying only for knowledge of His will for us and the power to carry that out.*

12. Having had a spiritual awakening as the result of these steps, we tried to carry this message to addicts, and to practice these principles in all our affairs.

CHAPTER 21
February 1993: Part 2

JUDGE WALKER HAD DECIDED SHE DIDN'T WANT TO HEAR from me, but I'd weaseled my way out of nine months jail time and back into drug treatment. The folks at Gateway Community Services had accepted me. I'd have to wait in jail for a bed in treatment, but I could handle that. Time in jail offered a reprieve from my addiction. Then, I'd go straight from jail to Gateway for another ninety clean days. I'd be safe. Jail and treatment meant some measure of security. I couldn't be trusted to manage my own life. They would manage it for me.

After three weeks or so, a bed opened up. I looked forward to the treatment facility and staff. I'd gotten along fantastic with the counselors and nurses. I'd no hope that they could keep me from using. I was a complete degenerate, but the place was nice and the people friendly, so I anticipated an enjoyable stay.

There's an old Yiddish saying, "Man plans, God laughs." I'd no plan when I went to jail. There was never a plan to anything so far in my life. After Judge Walker, though, I'd created a temporary plan, at least. I'd go from jail to treatment and that would keep me sane and out of trouble, a temporary fix to my life.

The day approached for my transfer. I was eager to leave jail. Upon my release, however, an officer informed me that I was free to go. No one from Gateway came for me. There was no transfer van or mention of treatment. JSO let me out of jail a day early by mistake. I knew it was an error and said nothing but thought, *Where's the damn door? We'll straighten this out later.*

Mitch came and picked me up. Rather than argue or tell the police no, I lit up with excitement. I was free to use again. I'd gone over a month without crack or alcohol. In the back of my mind, I swore I'd tell them in a few days that there had been a big mistake. For now, I was free.

I stayed at Mitch's house that night, giving him some lame excuse about having to turn myself in the next day. We drank liquor and got smashed. Mitch had no idea how my obsession with crack worked, that I couldn't drink and not want to use. Mitch and I had drunk together since I'd met him at nineteen. It was only natural to him that we toss back a few.

After I got drunk, the urge to smoke crack came over me hard. After Mitch went to sleep, I rooted around for his car keys but couldn't find them. I'd no rational thought at the time. Pure insanity. I'd gone through everything of my maddening past and still could not stop myself from going back to drugs again. I thank God that maybe he'd thought to keep his keys safe from me. I'd stolen his car before, so it came as no surprise. Unable to find transportation, I passed out on Mitch's couch. That night, I had my last drink of alcohol.

The next day, he drove me to Gateway Services.

February 18, 1993 is my clean date.

THIS WAS MY THIRD TIME AT GATEWAY.

I'd like to say that a sudden revelation came over me that first day in treatment—my first day on the road of true recovery—but that would be a lie. My mental state at the time was still about a temporary fix, about "easy time." I could do Gateway; I'd done it before. I could recite all the sayings and talk about the Steps. I could admit I was powerless. I knew I was powerless; that part was easy. I'd accepted my role in life: I was uneducated, an ex-convict, homeless, penniless, unemployed, and a full-blown crack addict and alcoholic. I knew that if they let me out of the facility, there was no way I could keep from using. I knew without a doubt that I'd no control, but I also knew there was no fix for me. Nothing could work. I thought I'd tried it all.

I'd reached my bottom.

At this time, my life was ninety days long. That was how far I could look ahead: ninety days, nothing more. It wasn't until several weeks into treatment that bits of light began to shine on me, a ray of hope here and there. In between those bright moments, I reminded myself of what a worthless piece of garbage I was. I listened to others share their stories but found it hard to open my mouth about my own. I believed I'd strayed too far and done too much bad even to deserve a better life. No one could forgive me. I was beyond forgiving myself.

Alone at night, my thoughts turned to the negative messages I'd received as a child and teenager: my father's assertions that I was no good, Grandma White's exclamations that I was just like my daddy. How could they be wrong? I could no longer use their words as excuses for my bad choices. They hadn't forced me to lie and steal and smoke crack. Lying in the treatment center bed at night, their voices playing on a loop in my head, I wondered, though, how I thought I'd ever be anything better. They were right all along. I was the proof.

One night, near the end of the first month, a counselor asked me to close a meeting. We all hung our heads in prayer. I opened my mouth to speak to God and could not. Tears welled in me, spilling down my face. I tried to cry silently, but my voice hitched and my shoulders shook. The years of shame and guilt and resentment and anger came crashing back. A space—I believe a space for my Higher Power—had opened. My heart could feel again, and the pain pierced me, more intensely than I'd ever felt.

A few nights later, a man named Tom handed me a Third-Step prayer card. I thanked him and slid the card into my jeans' pocket. Later in my room, I got down on my knees—in a way I hadn't since I was a child— and recited the Third-Step prayer, published in *Alcoholics Anonymous*:

"'God, I offer myself to Thee—to build with me and to do with me as Thou wilt. Relieve me of the bondage of self, that I may better do Thy will. Take away my difficulties, that victory over them may bear witness to those I would help of Thy Power, Thy Love, and Thy Way of life. May I do Thy will always!'"

On my knees, I turned my will and my life over to the God of my understanding. My concept of God has grown and matured since that night, but the same impulse has been with me from that first time on my knees in recovery: to practice the will of God to the best of my ability and in all my affairs.

As I continued at Gateway, I began and ended each day on my knees reciting the Third-Step prayer. I prayed off the card just as the prayer is written, removing and adding nothing. I'd come into recovery ready to admit my powerlessness over drugs and alcohol as Step One states in *Narcotics Anonymous*: "We admitted we were powerless over our addictions, that our lives had become unmanageable." Though my addiction included alcohol as well as drugs made no difference. I was an addict, plain and simple. I was powerless and my life unmanageable; my inability to stop and the insanity of my life showed me this.

Step Two came as easily to me as the first step: "We came to believe that a Power greater than ourselves could restore us to sanity." If I was powerless over drugs and alcohol and my life unmanageable, then something greater than me was my only hope. As I sat in meeting after meeting, I began to feel that there was hope. Perhaps all was not lost. Maybe I had not gone too far. Maybe with the power and love of a Higher Power, there was no "too far gone."

At that time, my Higher Power was my sponsor, Jimmy C., and the fellowship of the Twelve-Step program. I'd always believed in God, but in the very beginning I focused on Jimmy and the others in the room that I could see had made a transformation. It was a big step for me, trusting in Jimmy and the Fellowship. Jimmy had been my sponsor before, during my first attempt at recovery in 1989, and I didn't want to disappointment him again. Every day, he would tell me that I could do it, that recovery was possible for me. I clung to his words, believing—even when doubts and fears crept in. Jimmy and the others in the rooms had done it. I was getting to know people for whom recovery had worked. That bit of real evidence seemed a miracle to me, and I wanted a miracle of my own.

Step Three was a vocal admission of the necessity of God's will: "We made a decision to turn our will and our lives over to the care of God *as we understood Him*." When I say that I turned my will and my life over to God, I don't wish to imply that the heavens opened and I had some majestic transformation. It wasn't like that for me. I was at a point of such desperation that left to my own will, I knew I would use again. Mine was an incremental transformation, no less miraculous but not as dramatic and spectacular as one might see in a stage show. I prayed on my knees honestly and humbly, and I was changed.

Step Three took more, however, than a series of nights on my knees praying off a card. As my awareness of the Steps grew, I came to realize the power behind the words. Giving up my self-will and self-serving behavior, practicing a life that meant asking for God's will to be done, and looking for direction through God proved tougher than I could have ever imagined. Battling with anger, resentment, and depression often left me exhausted and confused. I turned to prayer each day to help me understand God's plan for me and for the strength to stay clean—for one day at a time.

Friendship is born at that moment when
one person says to another "What! You,
too? I thought I was the only one."
C.S. LEWIS

CHAPTER 22
Little Miracles

NINETY DAYS CAME AND WENT QUICKLY. AT THE END OF treatment at Gateway Services, I faced the realization that I'd no place to go. I could have gone back to my mother's, perhaps to Mitch's house, but I felt safe and secure at the treatment facility. They agreed to let me stay three more months. My oldest brother, Pete, got me construction work on the navy base, and I paid fifty dollars a week for my room.

My recovery continued, as well. I began earnestly participating in treatment, completing writing activities according to the directions of my treatment counselors. I'd never written much about my addiction, some during my first stay in Gateway, but never to this extent. It felt good to examine the ways in which my addiction had affected my life. I took account of my moral shortcomings and character defects in order to have my Higher Power remove them and find a new way of living.

By that time, I'd already reconnected with my sponsor from my first time in treatment in 1989. I first met Jimmy C. while working for a roofing company at the age of eighteen. He worked as a painter for the company.

Bent over cleaning a paintbrush, Jimmy looked up at me and said, "Hey, man, if you ever want any weed or anything like that, let me know."

I started buying quarter-pounds of pot from him on Fridays. We weren't friends or anything. He was just my pot dealer.

One day, I called him and he said, "I got popped!"

I thought he said, "*I got pot*," to which I replied, "Yeah, man, I want to get some pot."

What Jimmy was trying to tell me was that the police had arrested him for selling marijuana. When I realized what he meant, I hung up the phone and never called again. He ended up going to the Jacksonville Correctional Institution, which has since been renamed the Montgomery Correctional Center and is commonly referred to as "The P-Farm" for its earliest designation as the City Prison Farm. Jimmy spent a year, give or take a month or two, at the P-Farm.

In 1989, I attended a Twelve-Step program convention, running into Jimmy. To my utter surprise, he was attending the convention as well. He'd been clean eighteen months by that time. We talked about the way in which he'd changed his life, and I asked him to be my sponsor. When I relapsed six months later, I stopped talking with him. Before I broke off communication, though, I'd written him a bad check for sixty dollars. I thought it likely I'd never see him again. It would be no exaggeration to say I was relieved and thrilled to see him four years later, still clean, at a Twelve-Step meeting. I considered it a sign from God that I was on the right path. I asked Jimmy to be my sponsor again, and he accepted.

I think what made the second time with Jimmy as my sponsor different from the first was that this time I felt true humility. I'd been sincere in my asking the first time, but now life had taken me to a dark place where all pride and ego had been stripped away. Remarkably, I felt grateful for this stripping away—maybe not at first but before too long into the recovery process. Coming to Jimmy without my puffed-up pride and self-seeking ego allowed me to get real, to recognize honestly to myself, to God, and to him that I would do anything asked of me to stay clean. And Jimmy did ask this of me.

I'd pulled him aside after the Twelve-Step meeting, determined to ask him to be my sponsor again. "I'll do anything you ask me to do," I said.

Jimmy looked me squarely in the eyes. "I want you to call me every day."

"I will."

"I want you to go to a meeting every day," he said.

"I will. I'll do it."

"I want you to join a home group. I want you to make this your life." Jimmy touched me on the shoulder. "You can do this, but you have to have the willingness to take my suggestions."

Feeling his arm on my shoulder filled me with hope. "I will, man. I'm ready."

Relief washed over me when he said yes, he'd agree to be my sponsor a second time. Knowing that I had a familiar face, someone who knew what it was like—had been where I had been, done what I had done—gave me strength and hope in a way that cannot be understated. Jimmy and I spoke the same language. He got me. I could be real with him and him with me. Jimmy has since passed away, but I credit him with much of my early recovery. Honestly, I don't know if I would have made it without him.

Besides agreeing to be my sponsor, Jimmy took me to an event early on in my recovery, one that helped me further cement my relationship with others in the program, a camping event called "Bake by the Lake." I was between sixty and ninety days clean. Scott, another person important to my early days in recovery, joined us at the Bake. Scott had one year of recovery. Someone staying clean a year or two seemed remarkable, almost unbelievable, to me. I wanted what they had. At that time, Jimmy had over five years clean, which seemed too much to comprehend, but seeing folks who'd gotten through their first years set a picture in my mind of how I might do the same thing.

At the lake, Jimmy, Scott, and I shared our experiences with others who had similar stories. It was crucial to hear others' stories: their fears and pains, their hopes and dreams. For so long, I'd felt on the outside of life. Now, I was beginning to feel included, a part of things. My days clean were few, but, day by day, I felt stronger. Each time I came back to a meeting, I was more solid in my recovery.

After the first six months clean, my body recovered. I put on weight and began to feel normal—better than normal. However, guilt and remorse for what I'd done to others—to some that I knew, to some who were strangers—flooded my thoughts. I'd been relieved to go back to jail and then to treatment, to have been stopped before I'd committed greater crimes. I'd shoplifted, committed check fraud, rolled johns, broken into cars and homes. I'd even gone so far as to plan a home invasion. Thankfully, I'd been too afraid of the police catching me to see it through. I needed to be stopped. I wouldn't have stopped on my own. The severity of what I'd done nearly overwhelmed me, and I wished to erase the memories, but I could not. Not only could I not forget, recovery would mean taking a realistic account of my character and admitting my wrongdoings.

Step Four directs the addict to examine the past, exploring the ways in which he or she has caused harm to others and to oneself: "We made a searching and fearless moral inventory of ourselves." Step Five requires the addict to read his or her Fourth-Step inventory to another person: "We admitted to God, to ourselves, and to another human being the exact nature of our wrongs." My other person was Jimmy. The therapeutic value of one addict helping another is powerful and transformative. With Jimmy, I could not shrink from what I had done, nor could I let it consume me. With each passing month, our relationship grew, and I developed a strong trust in him.

Completing Steps Four and Five were difficult. They required courage and trust in God and another person. I had trusted drugs and alcohol, thought they were helping me cope and deal with life's issues. Now, I had to trust in God and my sponsor. Such faith, and the trust that it builds, is another of the blessings of the Twelve-Step program. Jimmy and prayer, especially the Third-Step prayer, made it possible for me move forward in my recovery. As we got down on our knees together in Jimmy's living room, I asked God for the strength to discuss openly my defects with my sponsor.

I had to face certain facts about myself. I'd been sick—mentally, physically, and spiritually. To get well, I had to take a hard, honest look within myself. I could not hold on to the resentments of my past. I had to let go of my anger at my father and disappointment with my upbringing. In working Step Five—sharing with Jimmy my Step-Four work—I recognized the pain and hardship in my family members' lives and better understood their difficulties. To recover, I would need to put my regrets, resentments, and fears to rest. Even further, I'd need to face the truth about myself, about my selfish, self-seeking mentality that kept me sick. I would need to acknowledge the role I played in my own choices and behaviors. My Fourth and Fifth Steps gave me the courage and way to come to these vital understandings.

What many call "working the Steps" was essential to my recovery. Everyone, I found, in the Twelve-Step meetings I attended had a story and many shared them, but if I was to make progress and further recovery, I soon discovered that I would need to work for it and approach my Step work with as much gusto and zeal as I'd approach obtaining drugs and alcohol. I couldn't let anything keep me from giving my all to my recovery. It wasn't easy. I found the program simple—but not easy, definitely not for me, considering the insurmountable amount of damage I believed I'd done in my life. Jimmy reminded me often that I only needed to remain willing and open. The God of my understanding would work for me in my life if I were willing and if I turned my will and my life over to Him.

Steps Six and Seven indicated my willingness to have God remove my character defects and asked Him to do so. Step Six embraces the willingness of our minds and spirits: "We were entirely ready to have God remove all these defects of character." In Step Seven, we ask for the removal of our imperfections: "We humbly asked Him to remove our shortcomings." This process of working through the Steps did not happen all at once. Jimmy guided me through the process, as I was ready, willing, and able to progress. I was facing the ways in which I'd been selfish, fearful, dishonest, and resentful. Doing so took time. I was grateful that I had the time to take. When I look back now, I see how these shortcomings had kept me from living a healthy spiritual life, which had led to my mental and physical deterioration and left me defenseless in the face of my addiction.

My Twelve-Step program gave me a new way to live. I had a problem, and its name was Tim. No easy fix could be found for my problem. I came to view and experience recovery as an ongoing process that was available to me if I would take it in and work it in earnest and with an open heart and mind. I would need to set aside my ego and pride, though, honestly, by the end I had little, if any, pride left. Or, maybe I had too much and that overinflated pride had kept me from recovering sooner. Whichever was the case, I'd become willing to step away from my self-will and self-centeredness to embrace a new way of living.

SMALL STEPS CAN MEAN SO MUCH, LITTLE MIRACLES ALONG
the way. I experienced several moments in my first year that kept me
going, gave me strength and even more hope that I'd stay clean this
time and not relapse again. One moment came in the form of a former
NFL lineman.

The lineman and I became friendly right away. I'd already gone through
the ninety-day treatment at Gateway and was living on the premises.
The football player was still in his first ninety days, which meant he was
required to stay on the center's grounds. At one point, my new friend
needed a check cashed and asked me to take his car and cash the check for
him. What an amazing request. Perhaps to him, it seemed like nothing,
just one friend asking another for a favor. To me, the act was momentous.
I'd come to a place where I could no longer be trusted. I had a long list of
people I'd wronged, some of them friends whose cars I'd stolen. I'd stolen
Mitch's car, one of my best friends. For this man who barely knew me to
trust me with his car *and* a check, that was truly incredible. I didn't want
to let him down.

It's funny to me now, but when I returned with the car and the money,
I half expected to be congratulated by the counselors. I beamed, handing
back the lineman his car keys and his cash. My new way of thinking
created in me a sense of accountability and responsibility for my actions.
I was powerless over my addiction, but that did not mean that I was
powerless to do the right thing. I could make positive choices. Such a
small thing may seem uneventful to others, but, to me, it was evidence
that I could be trusted, that I was coming back from the brink.

NOT EVERYONE AT THAT POINT, HOWEVER, WAS INCLINED
to believe in my recovery. I couldn't blame them, though, looking at the
wreckage I'd left in my wake. My mother and Grandma White embraced
my newfound recovery, but my father doubted that I'd change. At one
point, he looked me squarely in the face and said, "Son, you might have
all these other people snowed, but I know you're still using."

He would continue to doubt my progress. It would take over three
years before he could begin to believe I'd found a program and way of life

that could give me the strength and hope to remain clean from day to day. Sadly, he never found his own recovery from prescription pills.

During the first several years of recovery, I wrote often about my anger and resentment toward my father. His addiction had stripped from me the father I felt I could have had. Underneath the alcohol and drugs, I could see a man who had a deep sense of duty. I began to recognize his character defects and pain, how he was bound by his own difficulties. Though painful to do so, I struggled to find the good in my father. At first, I yearned to help him but, over time, realized my own powerlessness to change him or to make him accept that I had changed. The best I could do for our relationship was to spend time with him when I could and try to practice patience, understanding, and kindness.

Overcoming my hard feelings toward him, however, was not easy. To claim otherwise would be misleading. I struggled profoundly with my discomfort over having been born what I considered for so long "a mistake." I often said that my father married my mother "to give me a name." Looking around at other families—at children who seemed to be planned, anticipated, wanted—I felt cheated. He had not been a good father, but I wanted to believe that he'd done the best he could, and maybe he had. To his dying day, I believe he thought he'd been a good father. I vowed that when I became a father, I'd be the type of father to my children that I'd ached for and never had.

I'd been blessed, however, to have my grandma. My recovery was made even stronger by the love and belief Grandma White had in me. She passed away in April 1994, two months after my one-year clean date. Before that time, during my initial year of recovery, I spent as much time as I could with her. Her eyesight began to fail, and her health deteriorated rapidly. It killed me to see her suffer. I prayed for God to relieve her suffering and tried to remember that God has a plan for everyone, even for those who suffer. After she passed, I missed her immensely, but I was relieved to know her suffering had ended. I'm sure she's in a better place with my Uncle David and, today, my father.

Much of my first few years of recovery, I focused on staying positive and grateful—and I was. Not that I'm not positive and grateful now, I certainly am. Today, I have an ease and serenity that early on I still struggled to grasp. Times came, as they always will, when events would shake me. I overcame them and remained clean because I went back to the Steps, repeatedly reminding myself that I was powerless over my addiction and ability to control others. Again and again, I turned my will and my life over to my Higher Power. Though it was often difficult, I took a daily moral inventory—asking myself if I had been selfish, dishonest, resentful, or fearful that day. When I had, I faced my shortcomings, then asked God to remove them.

In fact, I found Steps Three, Six, and Seven a challenge. On a daily basis, I battled with myself against my ego and pride. Turning my life over to God meant that I had to set aside my ego and selfish thinking. Facing my moral shortcomings—and I had so many—proved a constant labor. I continued to pray, believing God guides me in my life and strengthens me. Times came when the best I could do was to hang on to the fellowship I'd found in my Twelve-Step program, the guidance of my sponsor, and my faith in God.

A particular time when all three kept me sane came when I'd just reached six months clean. I'd just left Gateway. Pete and I signed up for city league softball. My oldest brother and I had grown closer after my latest time in treatment. Softball gave me a way to release my physical energy and spend time with Pete. Growing up, I'd longed for a close relationship with my brothers.

All day, I'd been agitated. Thoughts of getting high swirled through my mind. I began to glorify the thoughts, recalling the euphoria of using. I remembered the days when I'd done just as I pleased, without concern for others or myself. A familiar and dangerous knot formed in my stomach. In my mind, I was relapsing already. I needed relief from that knot. I craved the drug of my choice and feared that I'd give in to that craving.

I made it to the softball game, but several innings in, the urge struck again, fierce this time. The knot doubled up and sweat formed on my brow. Without saying a word to Pete or anyone, I left. Dressed in my uniform and cleats, I drove straight to a Twelve-Step meeting across town that I knew would be just beginning. I made it in time for the meeting to share my turmoil. I'd been so close, on the edge of using, of making the unacceptable acceptable. I'd come so far. I didn't want to go back.

I looked at the other addicts in the room and said, "I want to use!" Then, I placed my head in my hands and wept. It was the most freeing moment I've ever felt. The knot in my stomach relaxed, then subsided. The craving was lifted from me.

By the mercy and strength of my Higher Power and the fellowship of my Twelve-Step program, I made it through the day without relapsing. I've never felt such a strong urge again, but I know that my ability to stay clean depends on a daily commitment to my recovery and using the tools recovery provides. After that day, I felt I'd truly begun a new way of living. Before, I would have given in to the urge. Now I had a way through to the other side. I regained a sense of sanity. I'd pulled the curtain back on the wizard.

IT WASN'T JUST MAKING IT PAST A DIFFICULT MOMENT, however, that showed me that I was learning how to live as normal people do. For the first time, I participated in "normal" adult matters. It felt as if I was growing up at last.

I remember the pride I felt when getting my first electric bill in the mail, as crazy as that may seem. I'd rented an apartment, the first residence in my name. I was thirty-one and, finally, doing what I should have done at nineteen or twenty. I'd never had a real service bill or account established anywhere in my name. Now, this document showed in black and white that I was becoming a part of the normal world. I stress the word *normal* because I'd never felt normal. The chaos and madness of my world had settled. I could predict from day to day how things would be, though I came to understand I could not control the future. I only needed to live one day at a time. I learned that as long as I followed my Twelve-Step program, my life fell into a rational pattern, a routine that gave me safety and security.

My first year in recovery, it became important for me to prove to others I wasn't the piece of crap they'd known. I'd felt like a failure and a loser for so long, perhaps I went out of my way to be sure people knew how well I was doing. At that time, it was important to me to have a nice apartment and car, to dress well and wear an expensive watch. Looking back, I know I put too much emphasis on material possessions and my image. Emotionally, I was stunted and sometimes behaved in immature ways, especially with women.

At the end of my first year, I began to feel that I'd taken my foot out of the door. Before that, I knew I was doing well, but in the back of my mind, I still clung to thoughts that maybe it wouldn't work. I could clearly see that it worked for other people, but, sometimes, I still doubted that it could work for me. Not all the time, but enough that I knew I was still sick. Picking up my one-year clean chip—or rather, in this case, a key tag—filled me with the confidence I needed to believe with all my heart and soul that I could do this. I could stay clean. I would always be an addict, but in recovery I could live the life I craved. Now, the craving was for everything in life I'd missed during my years of active addiction.

After picking up my one-year key tag, I went bowling with members from the meeting. Oddly, I ran into a guy I'd grown up with in Sin City. He and I had shot dope together. I'd no idea if he still used, but he didn't look healthy. I pulled out my one-year key tag, flipping it back and forth in my hand. I remember the look of confusion on his face as I told him I'd made it one year clean. Then, I shared with him how my Twelve-Step program had changed my life. That night, I also gave up smoking, taking a last drag, then crushing out the cigarette and proclaiming, "That's it."

Grandma White passed away two months after my first year in recovery. I'm grateful to God that I shared her last year on earth clean. I know she was proud of me. When we could visit, I saw the love and pride she had for me in her eyes. I heard it in her voice. She'd always been there for me, and I tried to return that gift as much as I could. It was finally time for me to live the life I'd always wanted. God had answered my prayer. He had stopped the madness.

As a single footstep will not make a path on the earth, so a single thought will not make a pathway in the mind. To make a deep physical path, we walk again and again. To make a deep mental path, we must think over and over the kind of thoughts we wish to dominate our lives.

HENRY DAVID THOREAU

CHAPTER 23
Relationships, Relapse, and Recovery

I MET SHERRY IN PROGRAM. I'D BEEN CLEAN ABOUT eighteen months. She'd been clean about the same amount of time and worked at a treatment center, bringing clients to Twelve-Step meetings. Her long, blonde hair hung down the center of her back in a braid, and her sweet smile cut straight to my heart. At first, she ignored me. I don't know if it was because she knew I was an addict and understood what being an addict entailed. I had to work on her slowly, and it took awhile before she'd agree to even a simple cup of coffee together.

I discovered working the Steps with Jimmy and in taking my Fourth-Step inventory that I didn't know how to love. I knew only how to possess. In short order, Sherry and I starting dating, going to movies, lunches, and Twelve-Step events. I spent time with her five-year-old son, though it made me anxious to think she might expect more from me in that regard than I could give. I wasn't ready for an instant family.

My feelings for Sherry grew quickly, but our on-again, off-again relationship took its emotional toll on me. We broke up repeatedly, often for no apparent reason. As she was a former drug addict herself, I thought she understood me and took for granted that her recovery was as firmly grounded as my own. Each of us walked our own path, but my naïveté about starting a relationship with someone who was also an addict blinded me. I didn't want to recognize the difficulties that might ensue and balked at the concept that "two sickies don't make a wellie." Truthfully, I was too new in my recovery for a serious romantic relationship, with anyone.

Our relationship was no good for her or me. Her sponsor told her she needed to stop seeing me, and she broke off our relationship based on the advice. After that, my insecurities, fears, and jealousy kicked into high gear, and I wanted her even more. Her sudden split with me, without any warning, fueled my self-seeking ego. I took the hit hard.

I wrote about my angst and hurt feelings, but the words did little to ease my pain. I knew I was unwilling to commit myself fully to the relationship. When she talked with other men in the program, my old insecurities surfaced, just as they had with Julie. I prayed for the strength to allow God to work in my life and clung to the faith that He would show me the right way.

With Jimmy, I continued my Step work. I needed to move forward. I'd hurt so many people with my past ways and needed to seek forgiveness from them and from myself. Step Eight directs, "We made a list of all persons we had harmed, and became willing to make amends to them all." I made my list, which was long, and considered how to make amends. I was willing in spirit, but facing what I'd done brought up tumultuous feelings.

How could I make amends to many of the people on my list? Grandma White and Uncle David were deceased. My father made it clear that he thought I was misleading everyone and continuing to use. Others, I'd no clue how to contact, or if I even should given what I'd done. Thankfully, all that was required at this point was the *willingness* to make amends. I prayed with Jimmy for that willingness, eventually coming to a spiritual place where I could begin my amends work.

Step Nine is very much an action-oriented Step: "We made direct amends to such people wherever possible, except when to do so would injure them or others." I began with my mother and brothers. I'd abused my mother's love for me, lied to her, and stolen money. I'd stolen money and lied to Billy and used my brother Mark's name with the police. Though I'd made no direct offense against Pete, Terry, or my younger siblings, Joel and Deana, my addiction had kept me from developing a relationship with them. I let them know that I'd made a positive change in my life and sought a closer relationship with them.

It helped me to begin my amends with my family members who I knew loved me and to whom I could safely and easily admit my wrongdoings, express my regret, and seek forgiveness. In my spiritual life, my aim was growing to be of service to God. I needed to live my spiritual life in action to the best of my ability. Gratefully, my mother and brothers showed me an immense amount of love and acceptance.

I made other amends as I could. In some situations, approaching certain individuals I'd harmed would not have been physically safe for me. Perhaps the amends that gave me the most emotional upset was my father. By 1996, his health had begun to deteriorate rapidly; his years of abusing drugs, drinking, and smoking had taken their toll on his body. Doctors diagnosed him with emphysema, and he went on an oxygen tank.

During my third year clean, he eased up in his feelings toward me and toward my recovery, admitting that he believed I was not using and that he was proud of me. Through intense Step work and prayer, I'd come to understand that he wasn't the monster from my childhood, but rather a sick man. Battling my own addiction, I understood better how addiction changes a person, makes them behave in ways they wouldn't have otherwise. I still wanted his love and approval, though. That hadn't changed.

As my father grew weaker, confined to his bed, I did what I could to help him and make him comfortable. I was all he had really. His early drug abuse had marred him and shaped him into an angry, resentful man who used guilt and fear to control others. Had I been so different in the throes of *my* addiction?

Spending time with my father in the last years of his life gave me ample opportunity to practice Step Ten: "We continued to take personal inventory and when we were wrong promptly admitted it." Step Eleven helped me understand how to interact with my father: "We sought through prayer and meditation to improve our conscious contact with God *as we understood Him*, praying only for knowledge of His will for us and the power to carry that out." I prayed for God's guidance, and He made it be known the way in which I should speak with my father: directly, kindly, and without retaliation.

During his last months, God provided an opportunity for healing. Lying in his bed, he looked at me and said sternly, "Son, you know I'm gonna die." I held back my tears. He continued, "I'm not scared to die. I've had a good life. When I do die, I want you to know it's okay."

To hear him say that he'd had a good life shocked me momentarily, but I quickly let it go. I'd longed deep within my heart for this moment. I stayed silent and let him finish.

Through labored breath, he said, "Me and you have been through a lot in our lives together. I just want to tell you I'm sorry for whatever I've done . . ." His voice trailed off.

It was the most humble I've ever seen him and the most sincere. "Well, Daddy, I'm sorry," I said. "I'm sorry for everything I've done to you, too."

My heart swelled with gratitude to God for giving me that simple, honest moment with him. Decades of anger and resentment subsided, my childhood not forgotten but no longer framed in the same bitter construction. My sore feelings healed greatly that day.

My father, Houston Ross White, died October 2, 1997.

BESIDES THE OPPORTUNITY TO MAKE AMENDS, ONE OF THE greatest gifts of recovery is the power and joy of service to others. Step Twelve directs us to spread the word to the still suffering: "Having had a spiritual awakening as the result of these steps, we tried to carry this message to addicts, and to practice these principles in all our affairs." Though I tried to be a positive example to him, I could not help my father end his life-long addiction to drugs and alcohol, but I could bring the message to others. Indeed, it is the purpose of this memoir. The honest and open recording of my story, along with my music, is one way in which I've dedicated my life to God and His will.

As time went on, I kept seeking God in all things. My addiction had limited my spiritual understanding. I had much to learn. Through prayer, meditation, and service, His presence became a real thing in my life. Service to others became instrumental in building my faith and a relationship with God.

When I was nine months clean, Jimmy took me to a meeting at the Lawtey Correctional Institution in Lawtey, Florida. Being back in prison unsettled me a bit, but in my enthusiasm to share with those who I thought might benefit greatly, I didn't hesitate to take the message to others. After a year clean, I began taking a meeting to the inmates. Bringing the message to addicts and alcoholics in jails and prisons became a passion for me. Shortly after, I started a Twelve-Step meeting at Gateway. What a blessing it was to return to the treatment center with a message of hope for a better way of living. In the faces of folks just entering treatment, I saw myself. As I reached out to the still suffering, I strengthened my own recovery.

Even as my service grew, however, I wrestled with my feelings for Sherry. My need to control others, especially her, still plagued me. I prayed for God's will to be done and for the peace and serenity that came with knowing I was powerless to make others do my will. Still, of all the people I reached out to help, Sherry was the one person on which I wanted most to have a positive effect. When she relapsed on cocaine, I encouraged her to attend meetings and continue to pray for guidance. Many nights, I prayed for her to find her way back to recovery and for me to receive the strength to help her in whatever way God wanted.

We'd both been clean several years by that time and had realized that dating one another wasn't working, but we'd continued to be friends. The break in contact recommended by her sponsor, however, didn't last long. Though we weren't connected romantically, we were deeply connected emotionally.

I watched as she spiraled out of control. I loved her and wanted what was best for her. I wanted her to love herself enough to stop using and seek recovery again. Some days, I would curse her for her selfishness, as if I weren't selfish myself. Other days, I would plead for her to look at what she was doing to herself and her son. At times, I'd alternate between offering support and distancing myself. I thought of her constantly, bordering on obsession. I knew my attachment came partly from my fear of rejection. I was a wreck.

Thankfully, I had God, my sponsor, and the Twelve-Step program to retain my sanity. After some time, Sherry found her way back to the program, and we grew in our friendship. The second time she relapsed, in 1999, I questioned how a loving God could let such a beautiful, young girl suffer so much and stay so sick.

My spiritual education during this time progressed slowly. Now, I know better than to think that God would let Sherry suffer. Now I know that He is there always. We are free to practice our own self-will, and she was doing so. In fact, her self-will was killing her. God would work in her life when she honestly and earnestly sought him. He would walk through the door, if only she would open it.

At lunch one day, I pleaded with Sherry to join me at a Twelve-Step meeting that night. She'd spent the first half of lunch crying, rolling up her shirtsleeve to show me needle tracks, evidence of where she'd let some girl shoot her up. My heart sank when I saw the marks. I knew what a drastic step it was from snorting cocaine to shooting it, how much more intense the high.

As she got out of my truck back at the doctor's office where she worked, she handed me a card. I opened the card after she left. Inside, she'd written, *Thank you for always being there for me and being my friend.* It meant a lot to know how much she cared. It was such a simple act but meaningful to me. I threw the card away later that day, before going home for the night. I didn't want the new woman in my life to see that another woman had given me such a thing. Joyce, my current girlfriend, and I had been together for three years by that point. Though Joyce showed remarkable consideration and respect about my addiction and recovery, I didn't want to upset her. Why spend time explaining something so innocent?

Sherry didn't make it to the meeting that night. A few days later, I got a phone call that she'd OD'ed and slipped into a coma, just hours after our lunch together. The girl had shot her up again. When doctors informed her family that they could do nothing for her, that she was irreversibly brain-dead, her family chose to let her go.

I cried for six months.

I remember a particular time with Sherry, forever burned in my memory. We were visiting a friend in the hospital. We'd had a good visit, even though our friend was very sick. Leaving the hospital, we got onto an elevator. I don't remember what we were discussing before the elevator; I suppose death. As the doors closed, she looked at me and smiled. I remember the certainty in her voice. "Don't worry," she said. "I'm never gonna leave you."

Some roads aren't meant to be
travelled alone.
CHINESE PROVERB

CHAPTER 24

Down a New Road

THEY SAY THE ROAD TO RECOVERY IS SIMPLE—
but not easy. I know this to be true. I'm grateful to God, my sponsor, and my program for my recovery.

When Sherry died in 1997, however, many days I felt anger toward God and the Twelve-Step program. At that time, I was speaking at prisons, hospitals, treatment centers, wherever I could spread the message of hope. I brought the message to as many suffering with addiction as I could. What I couldn't do, no matter how much I wanted, was save Sherry. My grandma's death, I could understand; she was old. Sherry died at thirty-two, and, except for her addiction, she had no health problems. I begged God to show mercy on her, to let her rest in peace. If anyone deserved peace, Sherry did.

As well as Sherry's death, around this time I dealt with difficulties obtaining a state contractor's license. With my felony conviction, the state had stripped me of my civil rights. I couldn't sit for the Florida Construction Exam, which was one of the requirements for licensure. The news came a week before the exam. A cold, female voice on the other end of the phone announced, "Mr. White, we are rescinding your right to sit for the state contractor's exam due to your criminal background."

The decision floored me. I'd studied for months. I could understand their decision, but I couldn't accept it.

I had no "plan B." I'd hung all my future dreams on building a roofing business. Between this news and Sherry's passing, my world felt out of control. I prayed for understanding, wrote about my feelings, and spoke with my sponsor. Jimmy C.'s emotional strength and faith in me took me a long ways during my first several years in recovery. When Jimmy could no longer sponsor me, I turned to Lloyd, an "old-timer" in the Jacksonville recovery community.

Along with Lloyd and faith in God, what kept me from relapsing was a strong foundation of recovery. My whole life revolved around my recovery. My friends were all in recovery. I either attended or hosted several Twelve-Step meetings a week. To leave my recovery would have meant leaving my life. Had recovery come secondary to my day-to-day life, I would have used. I'm certain of it.

Sherry's death solidified for me how deadly the disease of addiction is, how cunning and baffling. Here was a person who'd had years of recovery, had been a sponsor, had attended many Twelve-Step conventions and events. Like myself, Sherry had been an active member in the program, and, yet, she was not impervious to relapse. My experience showed me the need to practice my recovery on a daily basis.

Instead of wallowing in self-pity and anger—my prerecovery behavior, I prayed for a way forward about the state's decision. God answered my prayers in the form of then-Governor Jeb Bush and the Florida Construction Industry Licensing Board. God doesn't work on our time schedule, however. It took over eighteen months for the opportunity to come before the governor and petition to have my rights restored. When the chance came, I marveled at the coincidental nature of my hearing date: February 18, 2000. I would be seven years clean on that date.

The clemency board allowed a petitioner to invite one person to speak on his or her behalf. I asked Jimmy C. to be that person. Going on seven years clean, Jimmy could testify to the changes I'd made, the person I'd become. Of course, Jimmy had suffered a lot himself over the years, especially with his health. He'd been on a liver transplant list for two years. We made plans to drive to Tallahassee, and I looked forward to making my case.

The night before the clemency hearing—at midnight, in a Tallahassee hotel—Jimmy got the call that an organ donor had come available. A man in New York had died; the man's liver was a match. I drove Jimmy to the bus station to catch the first Greyhound back to Jacksonville. Doctors performed the transplant the next day. I faced the clemency board alone, but Jimmy was there with me in spirit, along with my Higher Power.

I waited my turn as man after man stood before the governor and his cabinet. We went in alphabetical order, which made me one of the last men. Each man walked to the podium before the raised platform on which the clemency board sat. Ten minutes. That was all we were given to plead our cases. After ten minutes, a red bulb lit up, indicating our time was through. Some men had brought lawyers or family members with them. I sat alone and waited. So much hinged on my ten minutes. If denied, I might not make it before the board for another year, maybe never.

Finally, my time came. I wiped my palms nervously on my dress slacks and straightened my tie. A tide of guilt and shame washed over me, and I wrestled back my fears. The decisions had come rapidly, like gunfire: denied, denied, denied. I'd no chance. Silently, I said a quick prayer. I would do what I could, but the result was in God's hands.

As I stood at the podium, my legs shook. I placed my hands squarely on the sides of the podium. Governor Bush looked up from the folder he'd been reading, my folder, the record of my past.

Before I could say a word, the governor leaned forward and said, "Mr. White, you've had a troubled past."

"Yes, sir," I replied. "Yes, sir, I have, and I want to tell you something. Everything that's in those folders, I've done. I did every bit of that. I'm guilty. But I've been clean seven years today. Today is my seven-year anniversary. I'm a member of a Twelve-Step program, and I went through treatment. The person who did all those things in that folder, that person no longer exists."

The governor sat back. I scanned the faces of the men on the board, one by one. "Don't misunderstand me," I continued, "I could probably go out and create a whole other monster that could do a bunch of things, but that person there no longer exists."

Governor Bush asked me where I went to treatment. I told him, then answered a few other questions about my treatment and recovery. Then, the governor looked down at me and smiled. "Mr. White, I'm going to restore your rights, and God bless you."

I nearly fell out on the floor. I could no longer keep back my emotions. A floodgate of tears opened. As I walked from the podium, the secretary of state called out, "Mr. White, wait a minute."

Oh crap, I thought. I was sure that they'd changed their minds that fast.

When I came forward, the secretary said, "I'd like for this to be on the record. Mr. White, you are an example that people do recover and that people can change."

I took a moment to soak it all in. Exhilaration pulsed through my body. I called my girlfriend, Joyce, right away. I couldn't have been more excited and floated on a cloud all the way back to Jacksonville.

Things, they seem, never come easy. Not the things that matter most.

When I got back to Jacksonville, I soon discovered that though the clemency board had restored my civil rights, I was up against the Florida Construction Industry Licensing Board, who still had to clear me to take the contractor's exam.

I waited the few months it took to get before the licensing board, feeling positive that if the governor could see I'd changed that the board would okay my testing. Standing before the licensing board seemed just a formality.

Ten or so men sat around a large conference table. I stood before them, ready to tell my story of recovery. Before I could say anything, the man who appeared to be running the meeting said, "I'd like to put the board to a vote to deny Mr. White the right to sit for the Florida Construction Exam due to his questionable character."

My jaw dropped. "Wait a minute . . . wait a . . ." I stammered.

The leader looked at me sharply. "Sir, you be quiet; you'll have your time to speak."

In my mind, I freaked out. I'd gone this far. How was this happening? I'm sure the panic showed on my face.

"Okay, sir," the leader said. "What do you have to say?"

Immediately, I went into how I'd made bad choices and took responsibility for my actions. How I'd come from a broken home and never had a chance. How I'd gone through treatment and turned my life around. I'd been clean seven years. I described how I'd gone before the governor. I begged for the opportunity to show them that I deserved a chance to sit for the exam. An onslaught of words rushed from my mouth. I talked as fast as I could, saying whatever I could think of to change their minds.

At the end of my frantic pleadings, the leader looked at the other men around the table and said, "I'd like the board to have a vote. I vote to allow Mr. White to sit to take the contractor's exam."

The men voted and it was done. I could take the exam.

I passed the exam the first time. I'm grateful to God, the governor, and the licensing board for the opportunity to better myself and build a successful business that has supported my family, my wife, Joyce, and our three children over the years.

AFTER BEING CLEAN OVER EIGHT YEARS, WORKING THE Steps, and reaching out to others, I evolved my understanding of God and His will for me. My insecurities about my recovery and my past were replaced with the knowledge that I was okay. I finally believed what everybody else was seeing. I'd become a different person, a better person, one healed by the love and mercy of God. I came to understand what I'd heard many times in recovery over the years: "I wasn't a bad person trying to get good; I was a sick person trying to get well." With this new awareness, my God-walk life became even more important to me. I began singing in my church and became involved in my religious community. More important, I found a purpose and direction in life that I'd never had before. I'd found a spiritual solution to my physical and emotional problems.

Though I've had many moments of spiritual awakening, one of the most vital to my reconnection with God came while visiting with the brother of a friend in 2002. My friend Jason had worked for me for several years, after I obtained my contractor's license. I'd known him and his brother Jeff all their lives and had worked for their dad when I was younger. Though I was closer to Jason than to Jeff, I knew them both well.

Jason told me that Jeff had cancer. I knew he'd had it once before and recovered. My roofing business was booming. We were super busy. For about a year, Jason told me about how the cancer had returned. I listened but didn't picture Jeff sick, maybe because I knew he'd had cancer before and beat it. I'm not sure, maybe because we were busy and I was thinking too much about my own concerns.

Though Jason talked about Jeff often, for a long time I didn't give it the consideration it deserved. Then, from nowhere, a powerful thought, an overwhelming urge, came over me. I knew I had to see Jeff. For two weeks, the thought plagued me: *Go see Jeff.* I tried to set the thought aside but couldn't. I *needed* to see Jeff.

I told Jason that I wanted to visit his brother, not even sure why I felt so strongly about it. I knew he had cancer and was sick, but, in my mind, I still couldn't picture Jeff fatally ill. The thought to see him, though, wouldn't let me go.

The next day, Jason and I went to Jeff's house. I found out then that Jeff had just returned from the hospital. His cancer had progressed. In addition, he'd recently suffered a stroke. I walked into the back bedroom with Jason. Jeff lay in the bed. I barely recognized him, with his drastic weight loss and partial facial paralysis. He was awake and seemingly aware of us. He stared at us with one eye open. The other eye remained closed.

I stood back from the bed as Jeff's doctor entered the room. The doctor asked Jason and Jeff a few questions about how Jeff was doing.

Then, the doctor's tone got more serious. "Jeff, there's a few things we've got to talk about," he said. "When the time comes, they'll try to revive you." The doctor held up a sheet of paper. "I've got to have you sign this piece of paper. I'm going to put it on the refrigerator."

I knew the doctor was talking about a DNR order: *Do not resuscitate.*

"Because if they try and revive you," the doctor continued, "being your bones are so weak, it's going to break your neck."

My breath left me. I didn't realize how bad off he was.

"How long do I have?" Jeff managed to ask.

"Two, maybe three weeks," the doctor said.

From where I stood, I spied a Bible on his bed. I considered the strong feeling that had come over me the last few weeks as Jason and the doctor walked from the room. I moved up to stand next to Jeff, not knowing what for, other than to be with him at that moment.

As I looked at Jeff, a feeling passed over me. The words came from me as if on their own, or some force beyond myself. "Jeff, I've got something I've got to tell you." I reached out and held his hand.

Jeff lifted his hand a bit to my response and softly said, "Yeah, man, what?"

I bent down, so that he could see me with his open eye. Still holding his hand, I said, "God told me to tell you that he loves you."

Jeff's chest hitched slightly, then he started crying. Holding onto my hand as hard as he could, he lifted and turned himself toward me. Just a few inches, so he could get a good look at my face. One eye open, he looked at me through his tears. His voice quivered. "Thank you, man. Thank you so much."

My life changed that day.

Before that moment, I didn't know why I'd come. To see my friend, yes, but a stronger feeling had spurred me into action. God became more real to me that day. I'd always believed in Him, but I knew that I hadn't thought up the urge to go see Jeff myself. The feeling had come out of nowhere. My only answer could be that God wanted me there. I know I could have said no, said back to God, *I'm too busy*, or *I'm too uncomfortable*. I believe in free will. I allowed His presence, though, to be felt in my heart, and He told me what I was to do.

This is my own personal belief, but I believe God used me that day to bring comfort to a dying man. God sent me for a purpose. God sent me to tell Jeff that He loved him—a simple but awesome message.

Jeff passed away a few days later. I feel the words God gave me were His way of letting Jeff know all would be okay, that he could rest.

THROUGH MY EARLY ADVERSITY, ADDICTION, RECOVERY, and submission to God, I believe I've come to serve a higher calling. My life, which was once chaotic and unmanageable, now has clarity and meaning. Truly, I am blessed by God's love, mercy, and grace. Where I once practiced selfishness and self-seeking, now I practice faith and acceptance. My life is no longer lived solely for my own needs. I live to serve my God and help my family, friends, and community grow in faith and love.

I've had many more times since that day with Jeff when I've felt like a vessel for God's love and will. Believe me, this is something that I never thought would come out of my recovery, at least not initially. Likewise, I don't believe it's offered exclusively for me. We can all serve a higher calling and purpose.

My recovery allowed me to return to my original starting point. It has almost been as if I have returned to my grandmother's backyard, a six-year-old on his knees in prayer to God to stop the madness. The madness has ended. I walk the road of recovery daily with my God, my program, and my sponsor. The madness, insanity, and chaos of my old life have ended as long as I continue to walk this path. Truly, this is one of the many gifts of recovery from addiction: *the road is there for us all.*

No matter how far we have strayed from the path, no matter our bad choices and selfish acts, the lowest, most desperate and depraved of us can return from our personal hell. There is hope. There is *always* hope.

What if I ran?

Where would I be?

If I turned away when God reached out to me?

If I never fell down on my knees,
would I even be alive to see his plan?

What if I ran?

TIM WHITE, FROM "WHAT IF I RAN"
OFF CD *THE LONG ROAD HOME*

CONCLUSION
Continuing the Journey

A FEW YEARS AGO, I GOT AN OPPORTUNITY TO SPEAK at a local detox unit. I entered the room to find ten or so people sitting on folding metal chairs that had been positioned into a circle. I've spoken now to large rooms and small rooms, and the intimate setting that night—just ten regular folks suffering with a powerful, destructive disease—touched my heart. I looked around at their faces, some worn, all tired-looking. My mind took me back to my first time in detox, to the pain and anguish I felt. As I made eye contact with each of them, I considered how I was only one drink or one hit on the crack pipe away from where they sat. Now, each day felt like a blessing, a daily reprieve from the chaos of addiction. I reminded myself that bringing the message of hope to others helps me stay in recovery.

Two individuals in particular caught my attention: an old man and a pretty, young girl. The old man made me think of my father. The girl, who appeared to be in her early twenties, reminded me of the young girls just like her that I'd met during my addiction days.

I took a seat on a folding chair within the circle. The girl hung her head, only looking up after I introduced myself. "I'm Tim and I'm an addict," I said.

The air in the room that night was thick with the energy of suffering and demoralization. I could feel it. As I began to share my story, the feeling in the room shifted. Maybe it was the strength of my spirit as I tried to share some hope with them or the weakness that each individual felt, but soon each man and woman began to cry. I began to cry with them. The power was unbelievable, a power firm and true and right.

After I shared my story, the young girl spoke up, sharing how she, too, was a crack addict. She told of how she'd found herself in a crack house, being passed around from man to man, a sexual slave for drugs. Then, the old man shared how he had lost his wife and children, then his job and everything else that had meant anything at all to him. One by one, around the circle, others shared their stories—stories of pain, of loss, of confusion, of hopelessness.

I gave what I could that evening, hoping that the message might make an impact. On occasions such as this one, I feel like a vessel for God's love and the message of recovery. Not every time feels that way, most don't, but there are moments when I'm reminded that everything happens for a reason. I find peace and serenity in understanding that my own problems and bad choices have, in the end, some usefulness and meaning.

MY WAY FORWARD TODAY IS A WALK OF FAITH, INSTEAD OF a walk of addiction. Where once chaos reigned, now clarity lights my way, and my journey continues. I persist each day in seeking greater clarity, understanding, and compassion.

I spent years angry and resentful. I sought escape through drugs and alcohol. I clung to bad relationships and diseased thinking. I chose what I thought was the easy way and broke everything in my path—including myself. Looking to be "fixed," I expected others to make me better, for facilities and institutions to stop and correct me. There was no stopping me—until I turned to my Higher Power, my God. I am no different from the millions of men and women who have walked similar roads, who seek a way back home.

Today, my word means something. I take my role as an employer seriously and show care and concern for the men and women who work for me. I've been blessed materially, but that is the least of the gifts of my recovery. Along with God and my Twelve-Step program, my beautiful wife, Joyce, and our children are the center of my life and my greatest joy. To see happiness in their eyes, to hear their laughter lessens any worries or difficulties. Where before I did not understand where I fit in this world, I now understand my place and my purpose: to bring comfort and solace to those who suffer. My music and singing is part of that greater purpose, as is this memoir.

I've had so many blessings along my journey of recovery. Fifteen years spent clean with my mother is one of those blessings. My mother passed away February 11, 2008. Growing up, she continuously shared with me God's love. The years spent deep in my addiction, she showed me unconditional love. She did not help support my addiction, nor do I think she enabled it; without judgment, she continued to tell me that she loved me and prayed for me.

As I recovered and got out of my self-focus, I saw that my mother had done the best she could in her circumstances. I came to understand that when I was younger and felt abandoned by her, events were out of her control for the most part. She couldn't have done any better for me than she did. My harsh judgment had been unfair—understandable at my age but uninformed. Now, I knew better. I walked fifteen years of life with her and came to love and cherish her. At the end of her life, God blessed me with a powerful moment.

She'd been sick with stomach cancer a long time, but the end seemed to come swiftly. I knew she was ready to walk with her Lord and Savior. She'd assured me many times. Though I wasn't fully ready to say good-bye, when the call came from the hospital, I prayed that her last moments would be peaceful and had no doubt that she felt ready to go. Her intestines had collapsed and her blood pressure dropped, which meant she might go at anytime. I rushed to be by her side. My brothers and sister—all but Billy, who lived too far away to make it in time—joined me at the hospital.

My brothers and sister waited in the ER lounge as I spent a few moments alone with my mother. I held her hand and told her it would be okay, that she was going to walk with God.

"Momma, you lived your whole life for the Lord," I said. "You're going to be an angel. You're going to be with Jesus."

My mother looked at me with happy, calm eyes. She understood every word I said. The look of excitement and serenity moved me to a place I never thought possible. She looked into my eyes, childlike and accepting. I never knew a person could look so at peace at the end. She was an angel to me already.

"You waited your whole life to be with the Lord," I said, "and you're going to be with Him."

She smiled softly. "I know, honey."

I sang "Amazing Grace" to her as we waited for her to cross over.

My mother lived a life of adversity, in all areas: financially, emotionally, and physically. She had a rough road her whole life. Her faith through it all was so strong and so real, and she'd walked that walk so long that, at the end, she was at total peace and accord.

In the dark days of my addiction, my mother shared a vision with me, a vision she told me God showed her. In this vision, I stood at a podium, dressed in a suit, my hands animated as I talked to a crowd of people.

I was in jail at the time, talking to her by phone. I remained respectful and let her go on about what she said God had revealed to her, but dismissed it as religious zeal or wishful dreaming. I was a hardcore addict and criminal. There was no podium and crowd of people awaiting me. Likely, what awaited me was more years using, more stints in jail, and, eventually, an early death.

My mother shared this vision with others, our family, and her friends. She told me she no longer worried for me because God had told her that I would be okay. In the last nineteen years, I've been blessed to speak with many people about addiction and recovery, sometimes in large rooms, standing before a podium, and sometimes in casual, intimate settings, sitting face-to-face. Each opportunity has been a gift from God. I believe my mother's vision was sent as a comfort to a mother who prayed for her sick son, not so that I would think better of myself or for my ego, but so that her mind might be eased and her pain lessened.

THOUGH I KNEW MY MOTHER YEARNED TO BE WITH GOD, the night she passed, my pain and heartache crashed in on me. Returning home from the hospital, my wife held me tenderly in our bed as I let go the tears. I'd long since resolved the pain of abandonment and regrets about the childhood I wished I'd had; now the tears were of my mother's absence in this world and how much I would miss her. Joyce held me close and reminded me of where my mother had gone: a place of eternal love, peace, and comfort. Her words and actions soothed me, my balm of Gilead.

My beautiful wife and amazing three children are precious gifts from God and only possible because of my recovery and continued journey down the recovery path. Learning to be a good husband and father, though, brought challenges and pushed me to mature mentally and emotionally. My addiction stopped my maturation, in many respects, at the adolescent level. I struggled for many years—almost on a daily basis—with learning to give, facing my fears of responsibility and commitment, and building relationships built upon mutual trust and respect. With the women of my past, I'd taken more than I'd given and shied away from full commitment. I'd let jealousy and control dominate my thinking. Even in love relations, I was learning a new way of living.

Joyce and I met through a mutual friend in 1996. Separated from her first husband, she lived with their two-year-old daughter, Rachel. On our first outing together, Joyce, our friend, and I went in-line skating at the beach. I found myself drawn to her upbeat personality and beauty. The first serious romantic relationship with a woman who didn't have a substance abuse issue, Joyce was a breath of fresh air and a much-needed complement to my life. Over time, she learned of my struggle with addiction and attended Twelve-Step meetings, events, and conferences with me, never judging or belittling me. Perhaps what impressed me most about her was that she never seemed ashamed to be by my side or worried about what others might think. I felt strong in my recovery and shared that feeling with her. What resulted from my honest admissions was a quiet understanding between us of my troubled path and my present journey.

Of course, like any couple, we had our difficulties. My discomfort around children showed. I didn't know how to be a father. When Rachel cried or wanted attention, I reacted hesitantly and, often, clumsily, which I recognize didn't help Rachel and me create the strong initial bond that, deep down, I wanted. I let my fear, and resulting lack of willingness, hamper my early relationship with Rachel. To Joyce's credit, she never tried to force our relationship to advance faster than what seemed natural. Over time, our love evolved and my bond with Rachel grew.

Joyce and I welcomed our son, Cody, into the world on September 12, 2001. Still, I felt qualms about fatherhood. Joyce, Rachel, and I had become a family; now a son was joining our lives. My misgivings showed in regrettable ways, as when I sent Joyce to confirm the pregnancy with her doctor, even after two positive results with a home-pregnancy kit. Excitement and expectation filled my heart, but, deep inside, my uneasy and hesitancy sometimes got the best of me. My hands trembled as I held Cody the first time. A weight of responsibility and worry clouded my thinking. As time passed, the worry and fear subsided, but in their place, old resentments against my father and upbringing resurfaced, burdening my heart.

The recovery path is a continual one. We addicts are never cured, enjoying only a daily reprieve from our addictions so long as we remain spiritually sound and work our recovery. The birth of my son became a blessing in many ways, some not so obvious. Through it, I resolved any lingering anger and self-deception about my childhood. I came to understand that had I not been willing to admit my powerlessness over drugs and alcohol and had I not sought help from God, my sponsor, and my Twelve-Step program, I would have been no better a parent than my father had been. My children's lives would have turned out no better than my own. What glorious blessings are the gifts of recovery.

When Kaylin was born, I cut the umbilical cord, crying tears of joy and relief over her safe entrance into this world. My shaky hands had calmed, and I held her close, promising to her to be a kind and loving parent. Over the years, I have learned to be a good husband and father. It hasn't been easy. Like recovery, the way is simple—but not easy.

Today, I have serenity about my family life. In my children, I see three beautiful, balanced spirits with optimism about life and hope for the future. I can look back on times with my wife and children, on our family events, vacations, and daily life and know that I am doing my best each day to make their lives peaceful and purposeful. My recovery has allowed me the daily reprieve from my addiction to be the husband and father I want to be and know I can be by God's love and grace.

IN MY TWELVE-STEP PROGRAM AND, NOW, IN LIFE, MY peace of mind comes through my faith in God. It has been an amazing journey. I'm here to say that this journey and road to recovery is open to everyone who suffers from the disease of addiction. Anyone can take the message of hope for recovery to anyone who suffers, anywhere. There is a way to recovery. Millions of us have found it.

During my journey, I met many people who walked the recovery road with me. I owe much to their love and support. My enduring friendship with Mitch has been a cornerstone of my recovery. Not long after my third time in treatment, Mitch began his recovery journey from alcohol addiction. Along with the crucial role Jimmy C. played in my life, I've had several subsequent sponsors: first Dan, whose tough love kept me honest and accountable, then Scott, who I met in my early days of recovery and whose friendship I cherish. For the last ten years, my sponsor has been Lloyd H. One of the early formers of my particular Twelve-Step program in the Jacksonville area, Lloyd has deepened my spiritual understanding and been a solid source of strength and wisdom.

If you are currently in a Twelve-Step program, I suggest that you seek a sponsor who, as is often said in program, "has what you want." Then, trust that they will show you how they got it and guide you in good faith. If you know someone who is suffering with addiction, find someone who's in recovery to be an example for this person, remembering it is never too late.

Some other practical ways to help a loved one who may be addicted is to invite them to hear speakers on the topic, talk about recovery options, or hold a loving intervention with the assistance of a qualified professional. If you can, catch addictive behaviors early. Parents, do not buy into the excuse that it is "only a phase." Ignoring and wishing will not make the problem go away. Left untreated, addiction only gets worse.

Yelling, threatening, and nagging do not work. Likewise, we can easily fall into the fatal mistake of "loving" the addict to death. To enable the addict to keep using is only to prolong suffering and endanger the addict and those around him or her.

I offer as testimony that what worked for me, and I speak only for myself, is a spiritual answer found in a Twelve-Step program, a strong sponsor, and my Higher Power, whom I call God. I'm humbled by His awesome power.

Today, I am here for the man or woman who cannot see the light at the end of the tunnel. I'm here to show him or her that light. As I understand God in my life now, God has blessed me to be in a position to share His message of love. In His love, the addicted may find new life. We are powerless over our addictions, but we are not without hope. With faith in Him, we can recover. My sincerest desire is that the drug addict, the alcoholic, the sufferer of an eating disorder, those addicted to gambling, shopping, sex—there are so many ways to suffer from addiction—reach out to a loved one, a friend, a trusted professional, or a Twelve-Step program. Find help now.

If my story helps one person reach out, then the honest, and sometimes painful, telling of my personal walk through life and my addiction has been worth it. I pray that those who suffer find the courage to take the first step. I'm here to say that at the end of the road is a new way forward. It is never too late. If you are addicted, if you love someone suffering from the disease of addiction, I invite you to take my hand down that new road. I invite you to walk a new life.

God bless you.

ACKNOWLEDGEMENTS

To say this has been a humbling experience certainly would be an understatement. First, I give all thanks to my Lord and Savior, Jesus Christ, who reached out to me when I was without hope and gave me the strength to change my life. I feel this has been a God thing from the start, which includes Kimberly. I'm very happy she was chosen to write this memoir with me. Thank you so much.

Many people in my life have made such an impact on my recovery and walk with Christ. My darling mother—whose unending faith was a light for all she encountered— has been always at my side. My lifelong friend and mentor, Mitch Thurman, also has walked through this journey with me, in good and bad times. I've been truly blessed to have a friend such as you.

When I was sick, Jimmy C. reached out and offered what he had found in a Twelve-Step program—freedom from active addition. He loved me unconditionally. Without Jimmy, I'm not sure I'd be here today. Likewise, I thank Lloyd H., my sponsor and friend, for his utter commitment to continue in this journey and to live one day at a time. With almost thirty years clean, he continues to reach out to the sick and suffering addict who seeks recovery.

Also, I'm eternally grateful to Gateway Community Services. I thank God that there was a place for someone like me, to help start me on my recovery journey. I pray that it, and programs like it, will continue to be there for the still suffering addict.

There are too many names to list, but you know who you are. I truly thank you all, especially Damien Starkey, for help with my music, this book, and all his selfless encouragement, as well as the book's other early readers: C. Brian Ashley, Karen Duncan Ashley, Mabel Carnahan, and Victoria Lantz, for their valuable and honest feedback.

My journey would not have been the same without my brother Billy, who cried, prayed, and laughed with me through all the years. Thank you, Billy, for loving me until I could learn to love myself. I thank, as well, my siblings Pete, Terry, Mark, Joel, and Deana, who have each been there in their own ways.

As with my dear mother, Grandma White and Uncle David have passed from this world to the next. The love and support they showed helped guide me in my journey. For better or for worse, I could not tell this story without the role my father played. What addiction does to the addict cannot be denied. I hope this work honors his memory and serves as an inspiration to all who suffer from the disease of addiction.

My precious wife, Joyce, has been my sunshine for many years now. I thank you for allowing me to grow in my understanding of what loves means, showing me that I have someone who will be with me always, and trusting me to give my love in return. Thank you, also, to my children, Rachel, Cody, and Kaylin. Words do not exist to express how much I love you all.

Lastly, I thank my pastor and friend, Pastor Kevin Hale, for the years I've spent listening to and learning from his messages of God's love and grace. My understanding of my walk with Christ opened my mind and heart. Thank you.

*Dad showing off his
Confederate flag,
late 1960s.*

*Sitting in Mom's lap in Jacksonville,
Florida, 1963.*

*Dad and I dressed up for a picture,
early 1970s.*

*Living a recovered life and visiting Dad
and his friend in Dad's home in Green
Cove Springs, Florida, mid-1990s.*

*Sightseeing in Tennessee with Dad,
early 1970s.*

Dad and his favorite beverage, early 1970s.

Mitch T. and I at a 12–Step world convention in Baltimore, 1994.

My father and his wife, Carolyn, sitting with Uncle David and his wife, Ruth, on the porch of Uncle David's house in Jacksonville, early 1970s.

My happy family sitting on the dock outside of our home, July 2012.
Photo© Scott Burchard.

Just out of work release in 1981.

Drunk and high in the neighborhood of Jacksonville police nicknamed Sin City, mid–1980s.

Setting up a roofing job, 1981.

My wife, Joyce, is my sunshine.
Photo© Scott Burchard.

Uncle David with his wife Ruth, late 1970s.

Mom and my sister, Deana, celebrating Christmas, Mom's favorite holiday, mid-2000s.

My brothers and sister gather with me at my dear mother's funeral in February 2008.

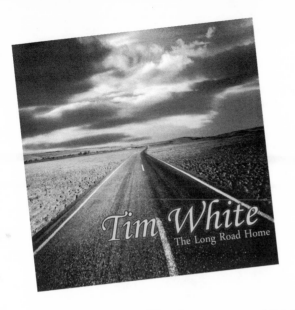

Experience Tim's message of faith, hope, and love on

The Long Road Home

Visit TimWhiteMinistries.com for upcoming news and appearances and to purchase the CD

Photo© Scott Burchard.